VAMPIRE STORIES

Midnight Hunters

Jo Sykes

Compact Verlag

Redaktion: Christina Neiske
Fachredaktion: Nathalie Russell
Produktion: Wolfram Friedrich
Typographischer Entwurf: EKH Werbeagentur GbR, textum GmbH
Umschlaggestaltung: EKH Werbeagentur GbR
Titelabbildungen: www.fotolia.com: Hassan Bensliman, DWP,
Julien Gremillot

ISBN 978-3-8174-7950-4
7279501

Besuchen Sie uns im Internet: www.compactverlag.de

Vorwort

Liebe Leserin, lieber Leser,

so packend war Englisch lernen noch nie! Diese Vampire Story kombiniert romantische Hochspannung mit dem bewährten didaktischen Konzept der Compact Lernlektüren.

Das vorliegende Buch wurde speziell für Lernende der Stufe B1 des Europäischen Referenzrahmens konzipiert. Vokabelerklärungen direkt auf der Seite erleichtern das Lesen. Jedes Kapitel wird durch abwechslungsreiche Übungen ergänzt, die auf unterhaltsame Weise Wortschatz, Textverständnis und Grammatik trainieren und festigen. Infokästen weisen auf sprachliche und grammatikalische Besonderheiten hin. Alle Vokabeln können Sie im Glossar noch einmal nachschlagen.

Viel Spaß und Erfolg
beim Englisch lernen mit Biss!

Inhalt

Chapter 1: The Forbidden Fruit 5
Chapter 2: Life Support 23
Chapter 3: Hypnotized and Horrified 44
Chapter 4: Midnight Hunters 63
Chapter 5: Hunting the Hunter 84
Abschlusstest 106
Lösungen 111
Glossar 116
Verzeichnis der Übungen 126

Zu diesem Buch

Auf einer Halloween-Party lernt Lorna den geheimnisvollen Warren kennen und verliebt sich in ihn. Als ihre Schwester Katie am gleichen Abend einen Unfall hat und ins Koma fällt, stellt sich heraus, dass Warren Schuld ist an Katies Zustand ...
Kann Lorna ihm das verzeihen? Ist seine Reue echt? Und wie soll Lorna mit dem unglaublichen Geständnis umgehen, das Warren ihr kurz danach macht? Hin- und hergerissen zwischen leidenschaftlicher Liebe und der Angst vor einer fremden Welt weiß Lorna bald nicht mehr, wo ihr der Kopf steht.
Als Katies gewalttätiger Freund beschließt, sich an Warren zu rächen, muss Lorna entscheiden, auf welcher Seite sie steht ...

1 The Forbidden Fruit

Lorna didn't recognize the werewolf. He was tall, much taller than Lorna. He had a powerful, muscular body and long, sharp claws. He was covered in matt brown fur and his eyes were the colour of blood. The werewolf was smiling, showing two long, perfectly white fangs, just like a vampire's.

He had not seen Lorna yet. Slowly, she turned around and began to walk away.

"Lorna!" cried a girl from behind her. "Where are you going?"

Lorna turned back around to see a black cat, a couple of witches, three vampires, a ghost, a devil and a man with bloodstained clothes and a huge chainsaw. They were staring at her. And there, standing next to them, the werewolf was still smiling with his huge white fangs – but this time he was smiling at Lorna.

"Another black cat! Great costume, babe!" the werewolf cried to Lorna. "Did you make it yourself? I'm Smithy, Ian's mate, by the way."

"WE made the costumes ourselves. Can you not see that Lorna and I are wearing identical costumes?" asked the girl in the black cat costume, the same girl who had called out to Lorna before. It was Katie, Lorna's identical twin sister. She turned to Lorna.

"And he's called Geoffrey, not Smithy, but he hates his first name. 'Smithy' sounds much cooler, doesn't it?" she added, laughing.

claw	Klaue
fur	Fell
fang	Reißzahn
bloodstained	blutbefleckt
chainsaw	Kettensäge
ϟ mate	Kumpel

It was Halloween, and also the night of the twins' twenty-first birthday. Katie had organized the night completely on her own. The twins and a group of Katie's friends were in a nightclub in Blackpool, their hometown, and the whole group was wearing Halloween costumes, as did almost everybody else in the club that night. The dance floor was full with ghosts and ghouls, werewolves and witches, who were all drinking sugary alcopops and dancing to equally cheap and tasteless pop music. It was only midnight, but people were already drunk. Most of the boys looked too young to be in the club, and with their short skirts and skimpy dresses, the girls' costumes clearly followed the philosophy that 'less is more'. Lorna was thankful to Katie for organizing the night, but it was far from her idea of a perfect twenty-first birthday.

Übung 1: Unscramble the words. Bringen Sie die Buchstaben in die richtige Reihenfolge!

1. Smithy was dressed as a flowweer ________________.
2. Ian was carrying a shicwaan ________________.
3. Lorna and Katie were tendicial ________________ twins.
4. At dimthing ________________ people were already drunk.

Lorna felt fed up. Apart from her sister, nobody in the group was a real friend. Lorna's best friend, Helena, was ill, and her other close friends had made other plans for the evening. So, although the dance floor was full of people, Lorna felt alone. I wish Helena was here, she thought to herself. And I wish the place wasn't full of teenagers. I wish the DJ would play some good music. And I wish it wasn't so full. And I really really wish...

ghoul	leichenfressender Dämon
equally	ebenso
skimpy	knapp
fed up	genervt
disgust	Abscheu
to wink	zwinkern
ϟ to lead sb. on	jmd. falsche Hoffnungen machen
overconfident	zu selbstsicher
mummy	Mumie

"So Lorna," said a voice close to her ear, awakening Lorna from her list of wishes, "Ian told me you're on the market at the moment."

It was Smithy the Werewolf.

"Sorry?" Lorna asked. "What do you mean?"

"Ian told me you're on the market at the moment," repeated Smithy, word for word. "You know – free, available!"

Lorna looked up at the tall, muscular boy in disgust.

"On the market? I'm not a piece of meat, Geoffrey!"

"It's Smithy, not Geoffrey! Anyway, what's up? I was going to buy you a birthday drink. What do you want? Another vodka and orange?"

"Thanks, Smithy, but I'm alright at the moment. I've got a full glass, see?" Lorna answered, holding up her drink.

"Please, let me get you one. Just drink that quickly. I'll get you a double." Smithy winked and smiled, showing his long white fangs. He was being a little too friendly and Lorna didn't want to lead him on. There was no way she was interested; he was too macho and overconfident.

"Honestly, Smithy, I'm fine," she replied. "But thank you anyway. I think I'm going to go and sit down for a while."

She gave him a polite smile, left the dance floor and walked into the bar area.

There were a lot less people there and she was glad to have more space. The music was a bit quieter, too. Looking around the room, it seemed that all the chairs and sofas were taken. A few couples were sitting beside one another, flirting and kissing, about fifteen girls dressed as mummies were sitting in a circle, drinking and

laughing, and a few individuals were writing text messages and shouting into their mobile phones.
"Aha," Lorna said to herself as she spotted a free sofa, right in the corner of the room. As she walked towards it, the DJ began to speak: "Okay, ladies and gentlemen! I've got some fantastic freaky music for you tonight, just for Halloween. Let's see you all on the dance floor!"

Übung 2: Simple past. Lesen Sie weiter und ergänzen Sie die fehlenden Verben im Präteritum!

As the next song **1.** begin ____________ to play, the girls dressed as mummies **2.** jump ____________ up from their chairs in excitement and **3.** run ____________ towards Lorna and the dance floor. Lorna **4.** try ____________ to move out of their way as they **5.** push ____________ past her, but she **6.** not be ____________ quick enough. She was knocked to one side, **7.** lose ____________ her balance and **8.** fall ____________ into a girl on her other side. The girl jumped back and spilt her pint of beer all over her own costume.

"Oh, I'm so sorr..." Lorna began.
"What the hell... do you... think... you're doing?" the girl yelled. She was a short girl with short blonde hair, wearing a little red dress and red devil horns. She was swaying from side to side and was finding it difficult to speak clearly; it was obvious that she had had far too much to drink.

text message	SMS
to spot	sichten, erblicken
to knock	*hier:* stoßen
to spill	verschütten
to yell	brüllen
to sway	schwanken

"Really, I'm sorry. I was pushed by another girl and..."

Before Lorna could finish her sentence, the girl jumped forward and pushed Lorna backwards. Lorna fell, unable to stop herself and too shocked to make a noise.

Lorna closed her eyes and waited for her head to hit the floor. She fell, and fell, and then... she stopped falling. Somebody had caught her. She opened her eyes to see a boy's face. She quickly realized that the boy had caught her with just one hand, and was still holding her up from the floor. Lorna tried to stand up. She wasn't hurt at all, just embarrassed.

Everybody must be looking at me! she thought.

The boy helped Lorna stand on her own two feet again, and handed her drink to her.

"Here, you nearly spilt this."

"Thank you!" Lorna said slowly.

Her glass was full. How had the boy managed to catch her with one hand and her drink with his other? It seemed impossible.

Übung 3: Odd one out. Welches Wort ist das „schwarze Schaf"? Unterstreichen Sie!

1. lady girl woman mummy
2. walk jump run speak
3. fantastic bad great brilliant
4. little red blonde black

relief	Erleichterung
hangover	Kater
to deserve	verdienen
deafening	ohren-betäubend
to blush	erröten

Slowly Lorna looked around. To her relief, nobody was staring or laughing. The aggressive, blonde girl was now arguing loudly with her friend, and most other people were dancing to the music. Turning back to the boy, Lorna added, "I'm really sorry if I pushed you."

"Not at all," the boy replied.

He seemed rather distant, as if his mind was elsewhere.

"I saw what happened. You did nothing wrong. That girl ought to go home. She's had far too much to drink."

"I know," Lorna replied. "I really hope she has a hangover tomorrow. She deserves one!"

The boy smiled and gave a small laugh. It was a laugh that meant 'I know what you mean because I think exactly the same thing.'

For a couple of seconds, Lorna laughed, too. Then they stood, smiling at each other nervously, with the deafening music from the nearby speakers filling the silence between them.

Lorna was the first to speak. "Anyway, I ought to go to... erm... to..." Where should she go? She didn't know.

"I'm Warren," the boy said, before Lorna had a chance to think of an end to her sentence.

"I'm Lorna," she replied. "Really nice to meet you, Warren. Hope you have a good night. But, like I said, I need to go to... Maybe I should..."

Lorna blushed. It was clear that Warren knew she was trying politely to end the conversation.

"Well, I'm going to go and sit over in the corner," Warren said in a friendly voice. "I'm tired of dancing. And the dance floor is too full anyway. If you want to come and sit down, too, you're more than welcome."

Lorna blushed again. This time, however, it was for another reason. The boy was extremely handsome! He wasn't wearing a silly costume, but a trendy grey polo shirt and dark-blue jeans. With his

messy blonde hair and hazel, smiling eyes Warren was without a doubt the most attractive boy she had seen in the club that night. And now he was talking to her!
"Okay," Lorna replied with a nervous smile.
The two walked over to a sofa in the corner of the room and very soon they were talking and laughing. And flirting, Lorna thought to herself with a smile.

Übung 4: True or false? Welche Aussagen sind korrekt? Kreuzen Sie an!

1. The boy managed to catch Lorna with one hand and her drink with the other. ☐
2. Lorna and the boy smiled at each other nervously and the room was completely silent. ☐
3. When Lorna blushed for the first time, it was because the boy was extremely handsome. ☐
4. When they sat on the sofa in the corner, it was only a short time before Lorna and Warren were laughing. ☐

Warren was happy. This girl, Lorna, seemed friendly, witty and intelligent. And with her long, dark-blonde hair and smiling eyes, she was certainly very pretty. They found it very easy to talk to each other. Warren was fascinated to hear all about her university studies in travel and tourism management and her ambition to live and work abroad after completing her degree. They talked about music, films and books. They even began to

messy	zerzaust
hazel	(haselnuss-) braun
witty	geistreich, schlagfertig
ambition	Bestreben
degree	(Uni-)Abschluss

local election	Kommunalwahl
spellbound	verzaubert
scent	Duft
to give off	*hier:* verströmen
intoxicating	berauschend
to trouble	*hier:* beunruhigen
to head	sich in eine Richtung bewegen, auf etw. zusteuern
to catch up with sb./sth.	jmd. einholen, etw. nachholen
genuinely	authentisch, echt
fake	unecht
shallow	oberflächlich

discuss the recent local election in Blackpool, before Lorna laughed, saying that politics was far too serious for a nightclub.

Yet there was something about Lorna which was even more amazing and beautiful than her hair or her eyes, her tastes or her personality. Before Warren had even seen her face, he had been spellbound by the extraordinary beauty of the scent which her body seemed to give off. It was an intoxicating scent. Combined with everything else, the scent almost made this girl *too* perfect.

Like a bright light, Lorna seemed to shine through his dark thoughts. A dark shadow from his past had been troubling Warren all day. He had received a phone call from a friend, Toby, that morning. Toby had told him that some old friends were heading back to Blackpool after years of living in London. They were a close and violent gang, and years ago, Warren and Toby had left their violent way of life. But maybe the demons from his past were finally catching up with him.

Now, though, with Lorna here, things seemed so much brighter. It was as if her presence could push the thoughts about his dark past to one side. In that moment, only Lorna seemed important.

Everything about her seemed so much more genuinely beautiful and cultivated than the other girls he had met in the club over the weeks and months. Though the truth was that this was exactly why Warren came to this club, right in the heart of Blackpool: He came to this club because he had hardly any feelings for the fake, shallow girls there. Hardly any feelings at all...

"So where do you actually..." Lorna began, but then stopped. Warren knew immediately what had interrupted her – he could hear the sound of her mobile phone ringing in her handbag.
"Excuse me a second," she said to Warren as she answered the call. "Hello?... Hi Katie... I'm okay... yeah, I'm just... what? ... Oh... oh right... yeah, I'll come now, no problem. I'm on my way, bye."
Then she turned back to Warren. "I'm really sorry. That was my sister. One of her friends has had too much to drink and is really ill. I need to go and help her. I'm sorry."
"Don't worry," Warren replied.
He was disappointed, and he realized that Lorna probably saw this on his face.

to judge	*hier:* einschätzen
to vanish	verschwinden
gentle	zart

"It would be nice to see you again… maybe?"
"I'd like that. So, erm…" Lorna began, and then paused and smiled. A moment's silence followed, and Warren simply stared deep into Lorna's blue eyes.
And then he did something that he never did in that club, or in any other club in Blackpool. He closed his eyes and slowly moved his head towards hers, hoping that he had **judged** the moment right. To his delight and relief, his lips met Lorna's a second later. For a few seconds, any thoughts simply **vanished** and he enjoyed the moment with this beautiful girl.

i
to give sb. a kiss goodbye
= jmd. einen Abschiedskuss geben

to kiss sb. goodbye
= jmd. zum Abschied küssen

Then, Warren moved back. After smiling at one another for a few seconds, he broke the silence.
"Do you have plans tomorrow? It would be really nice to see you."
"It'd be nice to see you, too... Then tomorrow evening!"
They exchanged telephone numbers and gave each other a **gentle** kiss goodbye[i].
Things are good, Warren told himself. I've got a date with a beautiful and interesting girl tomorrow night. Things are definitely good!

Übung 5: Passive verb forms. Formulieren Sie die Sätze im Passiv!

1. Warren kissed Lorna.

 ____

2. The mobile phone interrupted their conversation.

 ____

3. After a few seconds, Warren broke the silence.

 ____

Lorna was annoyed that she had to leave. She could hardly believe what had just happened to her. He was so handsome and intelligent and charming and funny and... wow! What a great kisser! Lorna bit her bottom lip, and for a second re-played in her head the moment their lips had met. She felt quite dizzy.

Although they had only spoken for a short amount of time, Lorna felt that Warren was everything she had ever looked for in a guy. She had been hypnotized by his hazel eyes and romantic charm, but she had noticed that Warren seemed genuinely interested in everything she said, too. And now she had to leave because Katie's stupid friend, Felicity, was ill! She could have screamed!

But, Lorna thought to herself, I have his phone number, and he has mine! Maybe he really likes me. I really hope he calls!

annoyed	verärgert
dizzy	schwindelig

She smiled as she walked through the crowd of noisy drunken people towards the dance floor. She began to imagine a date with Warren. The cinema? Or maybe a restaurant? The new Italian restaurant in town looked nice, so that would be romantic. Perhaps he would take her to the top of Blackpool Tower to watch the sunset? That would be amazing! She smiled to herself.

"What are you smiling about, Twinny?" It was Katie. 'Twinny' was a nickname the sisters gave each other.

"Oh, it's just because..." replied Lorna, and then hesitated. "I'll tell you later. Where's Felicity? What an idiot! Why did she drink so much?"

"She's going home now," Katie replied. "Sinita and Nick have decided to take a taxi with her. So don't worry, Twinny! We can still party! After all, we are the birthday girls!"

"Oh, I see. So I didn't need to meet you, really?" Lorna sighed.

"What's the matter?" Katie asked. "Don't you want to dance again?"

"Katie!" a voice called from the bar.

The two girls turned round. It was Ian, Katie's boyfriend.

"Does Lorna want a bottle of Cherry Vod-tastic or not?"

Übung 6: Fill in the gaps. Lesen Sie weiter und ergänzen Sie die fehlenden Wörter!

centimetres | army | bloodstained | muscles | seven | doubt

He was **1.** ______ years older than the sisters and at least twenty **2.** ______ taller. Lorna and Katie certainly weren't short, so Ian was without a **3.** ______ one of the tallest men in the club. His head was shaven and his **4.** ______ were huge, so his costume – a **5.** ______ white T-shirt, dirty jeans and **6.** ______ boots – was very effective. To complete his costume, he was carrying a fake chainsaw covered in fake blood.

terrifying	furchteinflößend
impressive	beeindruckend, imposant
uneasy	unbehaglich
thug	Schläger, Rowdy
craving	Gelüst, Verlangen

Unlike most people in the club, Ian didn't look comically scary; he looked genuinely terrifying, like some kind of super-strong serial killer. Lorna agreed with Katie that Ian's costume was impressive, but at the same time she felt uneasy. Ian had never killed anyone, but sometimes he really could be violent – not towards Katie or any of their friends, but he had a history of fighting when he was drunk. For this reason, Lorna didn't like her sister's choice of boyfriend. She wished Katie would find a kind, gentle boy instead of this man who could become a drunken thug. But Katie, not Lorna, had to make this choice, of course.

"Yeah!" Katie shouted back to Ian. "Buy Lorna a bottle, too. So five bottles altogether. Or does Pippa want one, too?"

Ian made an expression with his face which meant 'I have no idea'.

"I can go and ask her," Lorna offered. "It's no problem. I'll meet you back here in a minute."

"Oh *thanks*, Twinny! " Katie replied, and winked at Lorna.

Lorna smiled to herself. Yes, Katie has different tastes in music, mates and men, but she's still the best sister in the world, she thought to herself, and headed towards the dance floor.

What do I do now? Warren thought to himself. Maybe I should stay at the club a bit longer, here on my own. Or maybe I should go home.

Toby's phone call was still troubling him and he was disappointed that Lorna had left. Very disappointed. He was, however, optimistic. They had shared a kiss and Lorna had given him her phone number, so it seemed that she was really interested in seeing him again.

He was no longer interested in the girls in the club. For some reason, his moment spent with Lorna had intoxicated him. At the same time his craving for girls was greater than ever. Lorna was like the forbidden

fruit. Her scent was more beautiful than a thousand roses and her laugh was as rich as the sound of a symphony orchestra. Yet he could not touch Lorna – it seemed like that would be the ultimate **sin**.
In comparison to Lorna, every other girl in the club was boring – **plain** and **dull**. Usually this was not a problem for Warren. Normal, plain girls were uncomplicated. They didn't cause problems. They were easy to handle. But tonight all the other girls in the club were like aperitifs when Warren wanted a **feast**.
Feast. It was a tainted word – **tainted** by its association with Warren's old gang, the Midnight Hunters. Warren remembered the gang's leader, Rory, declaring 'Let's have a bloody feast, boys!' as if it were yesterday. A *feast*? Am I no better than Rory and the other Midnight Hunters?
There's only one answer, he said to himself. I have to leave the club. I have to go home, or people might get hurt. He stood up and began to walk towards the exit. On his way, he passed many girls – many very, very normal, plain girls. Tall girls and short girls, thin girls and plump girls, blonde, brunette and red-haired girls – every single one was so very, very normal. Warren didn't look twice at any of the girls dressed as witches, devils or ghosts. He simply focused on the electric green sign above the door. 'Exit'.

sin	Sünde
plain	unansehnlich
dull	langweilig, fade
feast	Festmahl
tainted	befleckt, unrein
familiar	vertraut, bekannt
artificial	künstlich

Then he smelt something. It was a beautiful scent, and a **familiar** scent. But at the same time there was something unfamiliar about the smell. It somehow smelt **artificial**. It was like an expensive perfume – powerful and rich but artificial, an imitation of nature. Warren turned his head to the right, and there, at the bar, he saw the girl in the black cat costume – the most beautiful girl in the club.
So it *is* Lorna's scent! Warren thought to himself. She's still here!

But why does she smell different? Are my senses playing tricks on me? It must be her! Her costume, her dark-blonde hair…

Übung 7: Comparatives and superlatives. Wie lautet der Komparativ und der Superlativ der folgenden Adjektive?

1. scary ____________ ____________
2. dull ____________ ____________
3. impressive ____________ ____________
4. bad ____________ ____________

"Hey!" Warren shouted.
The black cat turned to him and he walked towards her.
"Hi! You're still here! It's great to see you again. Let me buy you a drink."
A tall man with a T-shirt covered in red paint was standing next to the black cat. He looked confused.
"Who's this?" he asked her.
"I've got no idea!" the girl replied, laughing.
She then turned to Warren. "I'm sorry, but I'm taken. Can't you see?"
"But I thought…" began Warren.
Who was this tall man? Lorna's boyfriend? Had she just met him tonight? She hadn't mentioned a boyfriend before. And she had kissed him with such **tenderness**…
"Sorry," the girl said. "I've got Ian here. I'm taken, see?"
She turned to the tall man and gave him a long, passionate kiss.
Warren could not believe his eyes. This was impossible! Lorna had seemed so perfect before. Had he completely **misjudged** her?

He was shocked. How could somebody act so differently? It was really confusing. The different smell, and then this weird behaviour…
"Oi, stop staring at us, alright?" said the man.
He looked like quite an aggressive character and Warren didn't want to make him angry, so he quickly turned away. But still he didn't understand this strange situation.
"Ian, he's probably just confused that…" the girl tried to say, but the man interrupted her.
"Well, he can get lost and go and find some other girls to talk to. I don't want him near you. He's a creep."
Warren walked away from the bar. He felt humiliated and upset. Was Lorna just like all the other girls? Or was she worse? Did she enjoy playing games with people's hearts?
Although he was standing quite a few metres away from them, he could still see and hear the pair, thanks to his vision and hearing, which were much stronger than those senses of the average person. He decided to continue listening to their conversation.

tenderness	Zärtlichkeit
to misjudge	falsch einschätzen
weird	eigenartig
ϟ creep	Widerling
humiliated	gedemütigt
upset	*hier:* bestürzt, betroffen
ϟ to punch sb.'s lights out	jmd. bewusst-los schlagen

"I don't know why creeps like him are allowed in this club!" the man said, turning Warren's confusion into anger. "I can see why he isn't wearing a costume. He's freaky enough already! And he should be careful – If he comes near you again, I'll punch his lights out."
"No you won't!" the girl cried. "He might have been a creep, but I don't want any violence!"
"Okay, baby. You're right. Don't worry. Come on, let's order our drinks. I'll order six bottles of Vod-tastic. If Pippa doesn't want a bottle, I'll drink it. And I want a shot of tequila. Do you want one, too?"
The girl nodded her head, and the man gave the barman his order.

How dare she call me a 'creep'! Warren thought. Now he was furious. Full of anger, he watched the black cat and the man with the chainsaw buy their drinks. They paid the barman, then put the six bottles to one side so that they had space for their **shots** of tequila.

Übung 8: Unscramble the dialogue. Bringen Sie die Sätze in die richtige Reihenfolge!

a) He can get lost. I don't want him near you.

b) I've got Ian here. I'm taken.

c) He might be a creep but I don't want any violence.

d) Hi! Let me buy you a drink.

1	2	3	4

"Cheers!" the girl said with a giggle.
"Cheers!" the man replied.
The two clinked their shot glasses and drank their tequilas in a single **gulp**. Then... Bang! They **slammed** their shot glasses down onto the bar. The girl began to laugh. "Ah! Another! Let's get another! Another!"
It seemed to Warren as if that beautiful girl had completely disappeared. Now, he thought, all that remains is a drunken girl who thinks that I'm a creep! She's not beautiful. How could I have been so wrong?
The man bought two more shots, and again, the two gulped them

shot	*hier:* Kurzer (Schnaps)
gulp	Schluck
to slam	schlagen, hauen

down and slammed their glasses onto the bar. Bang!

"Argh!" cried the girl.

"What the... Oh my God, your hand!" exclaimed the man.

to stream	strömen
envelop	umhüllen
to resist	widerstehen
to dash	rasen, sausen

The girl's shot glass was broken and blood was **streaming** out of her hand. But this wasn't fake blood – it was the real thing.

"What have you done?" the man continued.

"I don't know! But I hate blood! Oh my God, it really hurts!"

Warren's attention was once again fully on the two of them. He had seen what had happened. But almost as soon as he saw the accident happen, he smelt the consequences. Blood. It was the same, beautiful smell as the perfume of her body, but stronger, much much stronger. The smell **enveloped** Warren. It made him dizzy with delight. His emotions had changed so quickly: confusion, humiliation, anger. This rapid change of feelings made him weak – too weak to **resist** the amazingly beautiful smell.

But this time, Warren thought to himself, I know the fruit isn't forbidden. There is nothing clean and pure about the fruit. It may be delicious, but it's certainly not good.

"It really hurts, Ian!" the girl cried. "I've got to get to the toilets. I need tissues! Tell one of the girls to come and find me."

And she **dashed** away and through a door at the side of the room.

"But wait!" the man cried after her. "Where are the girls? And what shall I do with these six drinks? I can't carry them all!"

But it was too late. The girl had disappeared, and the man was left standing there. He sighed, pulled his mobile phone out of his pocket, and pushed at the buttons, full of frustration.

Warren smiled to himself, then quickly, quietly and discreetly, he went through the door, following the girl. He followed her down a corridor and down a set of stairs. At the bottom, a sign saying

'Ladies' pointed further down the corridor. The girl followed the sign. She was holding her hand and Warren could see – and smell – blood **trickling** down her arm. The girl then began to cry.

to trickle	rinnen
to satisfy	befriedigen
to sob	schluchzen

Warren's hunger was now too enormous to control. He *had* to be **satisfied**. It was no longer a question of *wanting* the girl – now he *needed* her. He had no feelings towards her any more. She was no longer 'Lorna', she was no longer even a person. For Warren, she was now a drug – a drug that he needed.

The girl continued to **sob** and pushed open the door to the ladies' toilet. Warren licked his lips as he followed her in perfect silence.

Übung 9: Find the solution. Übersetzen Sie die folgenden Wörter, um das Lösungswort zu finden!

1. Lippe _ _ ☐
2. Schweigen _ _ _ ☐ _ _ _
3. eigenartig _ _ _ ☐ _
4. unecht ☐ _ _ _
5. Duft _ _ ☐ _ _
6. Verwirrung ☐ _ _ _ _ _ _ _ _
7. Entzückung _ _ _ _ _ _ ☐

Lösung: ☐☐☐☐☐☐☐

2 Life Support

"So do you come here often?" Smithy the Werewolf asked Lorna.
Lorna sighed.
"Not very often," she answered. "But Katie really likes it here, so I sometimes come with her."
"I think it's great," Smithy replied. "The drinks are so cheap! And everyone is here to party. I could come here every night."
Come here every night?! That sounded like Lorna's worst nightmare, but she tried to be polite.
She just smiled and said, "Yeah, it's really nice."
Lorna was looking for Pippa, but she wasn't with Katie's friends any more and nobody knew where she was. Now Smithy had caught her and it seemed there was no escape – she had to talk to him.

life support	*hier:* lebenserhaltende Maßnahmen

"Listen," she told him, "I should go back to the bar and tell Ian and Katie that I can't find Pippa."
"Don't worry about that!" Smithy told her. "I'm sure Ian will have worked that out. So where do you usually go out?"
"Well, to be honest..." she began, but then she was interrupted – her phone was vibrating in her handbag. "Oh, excuse me a second."
She pulled her phone out and found a new text message. It was from Ian:

COME TO THE BAR QUICKLY.

"It's Ian," Lorna told Smithy. "He's at the bar. I need to go and find him. I'll see you in a few minutes."

She quickly headed towards the bar. How **convenient**! she thought to herself. Ian has saved me – that conversation was **unbearable**!
Ian was standing alone. Six bottles of Vod-tastic were beside him on the bar, but there was no sign of Katie. Ian had a worried expression on his face.

convenient	*hier:* praktisch
unbearable	unerträglich
there is no point in doing sth.	es hat keinen Sinn, etw. zu tun

"Where's Katie?" Lorna asked.
"I was trying to ring you!" Ian replied in an angry voice. "Why didn't you answer your phone?"
"You sent me a text message and I came to find you."
"But before that I rang you about six or seven times!"
"Okay, okay, I'm sorry. I didn't hear my phone or feel it vibrate. But anyway, where's Katie?"
Lorna was starting to worry.
"In the toilets. That's why I couldn't follow her. She's had an accident. She broke her shot glass and cut her hand. You need to…"
"Ian!" Lorna interrupted him. "Why didn't you come and find me?! Is she okay? So where is she now? Still in the toilets?"
"I have six bottles here, Lorna. I couldn't carry..."
Lorna interrupted him. "But why didn't you…" she began.
But **there was no point in** arguing with Ian. She had to find her sister.
"Okay, Ian, I'm going to look for Katie. Just tell me, is she still in the toilets?"
"I think so... probably."
God, will Ian never grow up and take some responsibility? she wondered. Then Lorna left the bar and went through the door that led to the toilets. When she arrived at the top of the stairs, she saw her sister. Katie was walking up the stairs very slowly.
"Katie!" Lorna shouted. "Are you okay? What happened?"
Katie didn't reply. She was sobbing, but only very quietly.
"Katie!" Lorna ran down the stairs to her sister.

Übung 10: Antonyms. Verbinden Sie die Gegensätze!

1. ☐	impressive	a) rude
2. ☐	tainted	b) peaceful
3. ☐	violent	c) pure
4. ☐	polite	d) dull

"Katie, what happened? Are you okay? God, you're covered in blood. Is that from your hand? Katie, you've really hurt your hand."

"I don't feel well, Lorna," Katie answered. "I feel really ill. Can you take me home, please?"

Katie looked terrible. She was as white as a ghost and there were dark shadows around her eyes.

to moan	stöhnen
muddled	verworren

"It's okay, I'll take you home. But first we need to get a bandage for your hand. Let me look at it."

The cut in Katie's hand was more serious than Lorna had thought. "Oh my God, Katie, that's really bad. I think we should take you to the hospital – you might have really hurt yourself."

"I just want to go home," Katie **moaned**, still sobbing. "I'm so tired, Twinny. I just want to go to sleep. Please, let's go home."

Lorna helped her sister climb the stairs and walk towards the door. Then Katie's phone began to ring. It was Ian. Katie answered the phone and tried to explain the situation to her boyfriend, but she was sobbing and speaking in **muddled** sentences.

"Just listen!" she said in a weak voice. "I don't know what... it just... I just feel really ill, why don't you understand?"

This is useless, Lorna thought. She is in no state to explain anything.
"Katie, let me..." Lorna said, taking the phone from her sister.
She explained to Ian that Katie's cut was quite serious. Then she gave him clear instructions to find the club's first aid kit, get a bandage and meet them at the club's exit.

Übung 11: Forming questions. Fragen Sie nach dem markierten Satzteil!

1. Katie is **in the toilets.**

   ____

2. **Katie's** hand is covered in blood.

   ____

3. Lorna is taking Katie **home.**

   ____

4. Katie wants **to go to sleep.**

   ____

"Baby, are you alright?" Ian cried as soon as he saw his girlfriend and Lorna.
He was waiting near the exit, along with Pippa, Smithy and Katie's other friends. Katie nodded her head, although she looked terrible.
"Here, I've got this." Ian handed a bandage to Lorna.
In his other hand were three full bottles of alcopop.
"Does anyone want one of these?" he asked the group of friends.
Nobody replied.

"I'll take that as a 'no'," he **muttered** and took a mouthful from one of the bottles.

Pippa threw Ian a cold look and sighed. Lorna noticed that she, too, was not impressed by Ian's behaviour. Pippa turned to Lorna and told her that she had ordered a taxi.

"It should be here in ten minutes. Let's wait inside for it. It's freezing out there, and **pouring with rain**."

"I want some fresh air," Katie told Lorna. "I think I'm going to be..."

And she ran out of the door.

"Katie!" Lorna cried. "Be careful!"

She ran after her sister.

Katie was standing outside in the pouring rain. She had one hand over her mouth and was swaying very slowly from side to side. The two doormen at the entrance to the club were **sniggering** at her strange behaviour.

"It looks like Little Miss Pussycat has had a bit too much to drink," one said to the other in a sarcastic voice.

"They'll never learn," his colleague replied.

"Come inside," Lorna told her sister from the doorway. "You'll be freezing if you stay out here in the rain."

"Are you leaving, love?" one of the doormen shouted to Katie. "'Cos I need to **stamp** your hand if you want to come back inside."

"Come back inside, Katie," said Pippa.

She and Ian had followed Lorna, and they, too, were standing in the doorway, keeping out of the rain.

"I just need a couple of..." Katie started to say, and then paused.

Without warning, she collapsed. Lorna jumped out to try and catch her sister, but she didn't reach her in time. It was as if Katie had simply fallen asleep – she fell to the ground without a sound and then lay silently and completely still in a **puddle** of rainwater.

first aid kit	Erste-Hilfe-Ausrüstung
to mutter	murmeln, murren
to pour with rain	in Strömen gießen
to snigger	hämisch kichern
to stamp	stempeln
puddle	Pfütze

"Katie! Oh Katie!" Lorna cried.
It wasn't a huge fall. In fact, Katie seemed to have fallen quite **gracefully**. But still, she did not move.

gracefully	graziös
to rumble	*hier:* grollen
to glance	einen Blick werfen
instantly	sofort

Lorna knelt down on the ground, her knees in the puddle, and shook Katie. No response. Ian and Lorna joined her and tried themselves to wake Katie up. Still, Katie remained still.
"Help! Somebody help!" Lorna screamed in horror.
As if in answer to her cry, thunder **rumbled** gently in the sky above.

Warren was swimming out in the sea, not far from Blackpool beach. It was a beautiful sunny day. He could see happy families and friends having fun on the beach. Usually, he thought to himself, the beach is dirty, grey and lifeless. So why has it come alive today?
Suddenly, Warren caught a familiar scent – an amazingly[i] beautiful scent. A second later, he heard a girl's voice, back on the beach. Warren

Adjektiv oder Adverb?

an **amazing** scent
= ein unglaublicher Duft

an **amazingly** beautiful scent
= ein unglaublich schöner Duft

glanced over to see the girl throwing her long, dark-blonde hair over her shoulders. **Instantly**, Warren felt that he had to go and join the girl. He *had* to be with her, as close to her scent, voice and body as possible. However, as soon as he started swimming in the direction of the beach, the water suddenly started to turn red and get thicker. A strange mixture of emotions overcame Warren – instinctively he was excited, but the more real the scene became, the more Warren was filled with horror. There was no doubt about it – the water really was turning into blood.

Very soon Warren saw only waves of blood in every direction he looked, and these waves quickly became higher and stronger. He could hear the screams of excitement on the beach turning to screams of horror. But Warren could hear one scream louder than all the others – it was that girl, the girl he knew and loved.

Warren swam back towards the beach. He needed to get to the girl – to **comfort** her and be with her. Yet it seemed that the closer he swam to the beach, the redder and the more violent the sea became. He began to swim away from the beach, back into the deeper sea, and instantly the sea became calmer and the blood turned back to water.

to comfort	trösten
repulsion	Abscheu, Ekelgefühl
utterly	vollkommen, völlig

The families on the beach looked relieved, and began to relax. The blonde-haired girl was still there, chatting and laughing again. So once again, Warren began to swim towards the beach, and once again the sea turned to blood – this time much more quickly. Again, children screamed in horror and families ran from the beach, terrified of the huge red waves. And again the girl was screaming, not only in fear, but also **repulsion**.

Warren realized that *he* was responsible for the bloody sea and the huge, violent waves. The people on the beach were only safe if he stayed in the sea, as far away from the beach as possible – as far away from other people as possible. He was overwhelmed with a sense of melancholy.

Suddenly it began to rain heavily, but the families on the beach continued to play happily, despite the rain. The beautiful blonde girl was still laughing, too, but her laughter was becoming quieter and that beautiful, intoxicating scent was becoming weaker. Warren was getting tired of swimming, but he knew he had to stay in the sea for the rest of his life. He had no choice.

The heavy rain continued to fall, heavier and heavier, until Warren could no longer hear the sounds on the beach. He felt **utterly** alone.

Übung 12: Multiple choice. Welches Satzende ist korrekt? Kreuzen Sie an!

1. Warren was swimming in the sea...
   a) ☐ beneath a grey, cloudy sky.
   b) ☐ and above him the sun was shining in the sky.
   c) ☐ when a plane flew across the sky.

2. The loudest scream of all was coming from...
   a) ☐ Warren himself.
   b) ☐ a group of children.
   c) ☐ the girl Warren recognized.

3. When Warren swam away from the beach...
   a) ☐ the waves got higher.
   b) ☐ the blood turned back to water.
   c) ☐ the girl's scream got louder.

Suddenly he woke up. It was raining heavily outside. What an awful nightmare! At first he felt very **disturbed** by it, but Warren was happy to realize that it had been only a dream. Not reality. Everything was okay.

He slowly turned and looked at the clock on his bedside table. It read 11:27. Warren closed his eyes and started to go back to sleep. It was a Saturday, and he wanted to **take the opportunity** to sleep through the day.

Then, suddenly, like a **flash of lightning**, the memory of the night before hit him. He sat **bolt upright** in his bed, his eyes wide open in horror. Everything was *not* okay.

Oh my God, he thought to himself, I acted so stupidly. Why did I put that girl, Lorna, at risk? I could have hurt her. I was angry, but that was no reason to act so violently. What's got into me?

Then Warren remembered what Toby had told him. The Midnight Hunters were back. Was this all connected? Filled with disturbing thoughts but still very tired Warren decided to try and go back to sleep. He just didn't want to think about it all. However, a few minutes later his mobile phone beeped. 'One new message: LORNA' read the screen.

disturbed	beunruhigt
take the opportunity	die Gelegenheit ergreifen
flash of lightning	Blitz
bolt upright	kerzengerade
incident	Vorfall

Warren was surprised and, at the same time, a little bit worried. Why had she sent him a message? It had been clear that she had a boyfriend – or at least a man for the evening. Maybe she remembered her experience in the toilets? He opened the message and read the words on the screen:

hi warren its lorna. sorry i had 2 leave last nite. was rly nice 2 meet u. unfortunately i dont think i can meet u today. my sister katie had an accident & im @ the hospital with her. im sorry. i hope u have a nice weekend & take care of urself. love lorna x

Her sister? An accident? Something wasn't right. It was a good sign that she didn't mention the incident in the toilets, but why didn't Lorna say anything about her behaviour at the bar? Things suddenly seemed much stranger. Had Warren really understood the situation correctly? He decided he needed some answers so there was only one option: Although he had no idea what to say, he had to phone Lorna. He needed some answers and some clarity.

He found Lorna's number in his phone and pressed the green button before he had the chance to change his mind. It seemed to ring for ever, but **eventually**, someone answered.

"Hello?"

"Hi, Lorna," he said, "it's Warren." He paused for a moment and then continued. "Are you okay? I got your text message. What's happened?"

"I'm sorry," Lorna replied. "I didn't mean to worry you. It's just that... Oh God, I'm so sorry. I really shouldn't have sent you the message."

Had Lorna begun to cry? Now Warren was extremely **concerned**.

"What is it?" he asked. "Lorna, please, tell me. What's happened?"

"It doesn't matter," she replied. "You don't need to know. I'm fine. It's just my... my sister... my sister Katie. She's..."

Then Lorna's voice **faded away** and all Warren could hear was the sound of her sobbing.

"What is it, Lorna? What's happened to your sister? You said... an accident?"

"I'm sorry, Warren. This is embarrassing. I don't even know you. I met you in a club, and now I am crying on the phone to you. I'm so sorry. I feel really stupid."

Lorna's voice became clearer. She was trying to stop herself from crying. She **coughed** a few times and then started to speak again. "Yes, Katie had an accident. We were in the club and everything was fine until she cut her hand on a broken glass. She ran to the toilet and when she came back she was as white as a..."

"Katie cut her hand?!" Warren said, interrupting Lorna. "She cut her hand at the bar?"

Things suddenly became clear. The girl at the bar wasn't Lorna. The girl whom he had followed to the toilets wasn't Lorna. It was her sister. And now she was in hospital! What had he done?!

"Yeah," Lorna replied. "But it wasn't too bad. I don't understand why she was so white. But she looked *really* ill, so we decided to leave. Katie ran outside because she felt sick and needed some fresh air.

And then she... just collapsed..."

Warren didn't know what to say. What *could* he say? The words "I'm so sorry, Lorna" came out of his mouth. But Lorna couldn't realize how sorry he was.

Lorna continued speaking, but Warren could tell that she was finding the whole thing difficult to talk about.

"Then she was **unconscious**. She hit her head, you see. We called for an ambulance, and at the hospital the doctors had to put her on a life support machine. She's still sleeping now. We don't know if she'll... Oh my God, we don't know if she'll wake up! The doctors don't know if she'll wake up!"

eventually	endlich, schließlich
concerned	besorgt
to fade away	schwinden
to cough	husten
unconscious	bewusstlos

Warren was horrified. "I'm so sorry, Lorna." It was all he could say.

"She seemed so fine all night," Lorna added. "She was having so much fun. It was our twenty-first birthday! And now this!"

Their birthday! Now Warren understood the horrible truth: Lorna and her sister, Katie, were identical twins.

So that's why Lorna's sister smelt slightly different! he thought to himself. Why was I so stupid?!

"What else have the doctors told you?" Warren asked carefully.

"They told us that..." Lorna began. But then she sighed and her tone suddenly changed. "Listen, Warren. It doesn't matter to you. You don't know Katie. You don't even know me! I need to go, anyway. Thank you for your concern but don't worry about us. Honestly, we'll be fine. Have a good weekend."

But it was clear to Warren that Lorna wasn't fine, and that, more importantly, her sister was far from okay.

"Which hospital is Katie at?" Warren asked quickly, before Lorna could say goodbye.

"Blackpool Victoria," Lorna replied.

"Okay," Warren said, but he didn't really know what he was saying. It was like he was speaking faster than he was actually thinking. "I need to see you. I'll come and meet you there."
"No, Warren," Lorna replied. "Thank you. But no. I need to stay with Katie and my mum and dad."
"Please," Warren insisted. "Please, Lorna. We need to talk. It's important."
He was responsible, he knew, so he had to take some responsibility in sorting it out.
"Thank you, Warren. But no. I need to go. Goodbye."
Before Warren could protest, Lorna had hung up.

Übung 13: **Homophones. Lesen Sie weiter und unterstreichen Sie die richtigen Variante!**

Warren had to talk to Lorna. He thought through his options. Should he ring her later? But Katie's condition seemed so critical. What if **1.** their / there / they're was no 'later'? If there was something he could do to help, then he had to act immediately. He had to go **2.** to / two / too the hospital. Warren noticed that his mouth had become very dry. The thought of the hospital made him feel uneasy. He avoided hospitals. So much blood in one space! So much temptation. Warren **3.** knew / new that **temptation** was dangerous. Spontaneous, **reckless** feeding always **4.** lead / led to disaster.

Hundreds of people were killed each year as a result of 'crimes of passion' – jealous husbands, furious wives, fits of rage, uncontrollable emotions. No, there had been nothing controlled and planned about his feeding the previous night. Warren held his head in his hands in shame. Reckless feeding, caused by uncontrollable temptation, was no different – it, too, was a 'crime of passion'.
Warren felt guilt and shame digging their way deeper and deeper into his heart. What's happening to me? he asked himself. I thought I'd buried this side of myself years ago. I thought Warren the Midnight Hunter was history. Am I really the same as Rory and those other *monsters*? Is there no way of escaping the evil side of my existence? Am I doomed to go on like this – forever?
Despite the feelings of guilt and unease, Warren knew that he had to go to the hospital. He had to face his fears. He had to face himself.

temptation	Versuchung
reckless	gedankenlos, rücksichtslos
fit of rage	Wutanfall
to dig	*hier:* graben
to bury	begraben
doomed	verdammt
ward	(Krankenhaus-) Station
tube	*hier:* Schlauch
wire	*hier:* Kabel
steady	gleichbleibend
anxiety	Angst

"You look tired, Lorna," Ian said to his girlfriend's sister.
They were sitting in the hospital in the intensive care ward, next to Katie, with Mr and Mrs Irvine, Lorna and Katie's parents. Katie was lying on a bed, completely unconscious. Tubes and wires linked her body to a machine. *Peep, peep, peep*, came the steady, regular sound from the machine.
"I'm fine," Lorna replied.
It was simply the easiest answer to give – two little words which actually meant 'I feel terrible, and you know it, but I don't want to talk about it.' Everybody was tired, both mentally and physically. But they were overcome with anxiety, too, and this made sleep

impossible. Lorna was still wearing her black dress and tights, but she had taken off the other parts of her costume – her homemade ears and clip-on tail – and had washed off the face paint.

Mr and Mrs Irvine lived less than half a mile from the hospital, so they had arrived within a few minutes of receiving an urgent and panicked phone call from Lorna. Mr Irvine had shouted at Ian when he arrived. He had said that Ian obviously didn't take care of Katie well enough. Ian had shouted back and an argument had developed. But they had soon realized that arguing wasn't helpful, and now they were sitting quietly, each person lost in his or her own thoughts.

Ian interrupted the silence with a long, slow sigh. He was still wearing his disturbing costume – the bloodstained T-shirt and dirty jeans. Even without the chainsaw he still looked ridiculous sitting in the clean hospital ward.

He turned to Lorna. "Who were you on the phone to earlier??"

"When?" Lorna asked, turning her head only slightly in Ian's direction.

"Earlier. In the reception area. I saw you when I went to the hospital kiosk."

"Oh... Just a friend."

"Which friend? You looked pretty[i] upset. Were you crying?"

Lorna turned red with embarrassment. Why did Ian have to be so insensitive? She turned fully towards him and looked him in the eyes.

> **Pretty** bedeutet hübsch, es kann aber auch einem Adjektiv vorangestellt werden und hat dann verstärkende Wirkung.
>
> pretty upset = ziemlich traurig

"I was just a bit upset, okay? It was Helena. She wanted to know how I was," Lorna lied.

It seemed to stop Ian's questions. For ten more long minutes they sat there in silence, with just the *peep*, *peep*, *peep* of the life support machine. Then Lorna felt her phone vibrate.

One new message: WARREN.

i had to come lorna. i'm in the canteen now. please come and meet me.

"Lorna, you shouldn't have that turned on in here!" said Mr Irvine in a sharp voice.
"Sorry, Dad," Lorna replied. "I'll turn it off now. I'm just going to the canteen to pick up a snack and go outside for some fresh air."
"Me too," Ian said. "I need a cigarette."
"That's hardly fresh air," Lorna said in a sarcastic voice. "And you can't smoke outside the main entrance, Ian. You have to go to the smoking area."
This was convenient for Lorna – she sent Ian in the opposite direction and headed towards the canteen, next to the main entrance.

tights *pl*	Strumpfhose
insensitive	unsensibel, taktlos
hooded jumper/ hoody	Kapuzenpulli
to be struck by sth.	von etw. beeindruckt sein
gorgeous	toll, umwerfend
to swallow	schlucken
odd	seltsam

When Lorna arrived at the canteen, she spotted Warren immediately. He was sitting alone at a table, wearing a grey hooded jumper and dark jeans. His messy blonde hair was perhaps messier than the previous night, and he looked tired, but Lorna was once again struck by how handsome he was. Wow, she thought to herself, he really is as gorgeous as I remember. Even in a hoody he manages to look sexy! Immediately she felt guilty for having such thoughts while Katie was so very ill upstairs in the hospital.
"Hi," Warren said to Lorna when she was seated.
She noticed that he swallowed, as if her arrival made him feel uneasy. "What do you want to drink? A coffee?"
"Hi... Erm... No, thanks," Lorna answered with a small smile.
It felt odd to see this handsome boy, whom she had kissed only the night before, in such a strange situation.
"I'm not thirsty."
"Me neither," Warren replied.

Übung 14: Crossword. Lösen Sie das Kreuzworträtsel!

Down

1. A short communication to give someone information.
3. A mother or father.
4. The organ which pumps blood around the body.

Across

2. A female partner.
4. A place to receive medical care and treatment.
5. An act which breaks the law.
6. 365 days.
7. The part of the body we use to hear.

"Warren," Lorna started, then hesitated, searching for the most polite way to get her message across. The last thing she wanted to do was **offend** him. "I really **appreciate** your concern, and I'm sorry to worry you. But you don't need to be here."

"Please, don't apologize. I'm glad you told me. And I *did* need to come. We need to talk. God, you must be **exhausted**."

She gave him a small smile. Is it that obvious? she asked herself. I suppose if my eyes look as heavy as they feel then it must be.

to offend	beleidigen
to appreciate	schätzen, zu schätzen wissen
exhausted	erschöpft
curiously	neugierig

"I'm fine." She paused for a few seconds. "So... What do you want to talk about?"
Warren seemed to hesitate. Lorna noticed that he looked uncomfortable and that he kept glancing around.
"I just need to know that your sister's going to be okay," he said, finally.
"Warren, listen. The doctors don't know if she's going to be okay. Katie's very ill. There's not much more I can tell you. I would really like to see you again, honestly, Warren, but not now."
"The doctors don't know?" Warren repeated, seeming to ignore her last comment.
"No, they don't understand why Katie's fall was so serious. She lost an awful lot of blood last night, but they don't understand why. She didn't fall far and her cut wasn't that serious. They gave her a blood transfusion straight away. That saved her life." Lorna paused for a few seconds then added, "But now we don't know if she will wake up."
Now Warren seemed particularly quiet.
"What's the matter?" she asked.
Warren remained silent for a few more seconds, and then slowly replied, "I'm sorry. I don't know exactly how, but I want to help. You need to let me know if Katie's condition gets worse."
Lorna was beginning to get frustrated. Warren had seemed so intelligent the previous night – why didn't he understand? If the doctors couldn't put things right, then how on earth did he think he could!
"You don't need to be sorry. You're not responsible."
"No, you're right," Warren muttered, then swallowed. "I'm not... Oh, God." He coughed into his hand.
"What is it?" Lorna asked curiously. Why was he reacting so oddly? "Is there something you're not telling me?"
"Listen, Lorna. You wouldn't understand. You just need to tell me if anything happens. Then I can undo the..." He sighed.

suspicious	*hier:* misstrauisch
↯ to get it	etw. kapieren
to fail to do sth.	etw. versäumen, etw. nicht tun
to run riot	durchdrehen, verrücktspielen
despair	Verzweiflung
chest	Brust(korb)

Lorna was beginning to get suspicious. What did he mean by 'undo'? "Warren, I don't get it. It's not like you caused her accident!"
Warren simply coughed and turned his head away. Lorna's heart began to race and she suddenly felt cold. What the hell was he hiding from her?
"Warren," she said directly, forcing him to make eye contact with her. "Give me a straight answer. You didn't hurt Katie, did you?"
Warren didn't say a word, and after a second, he looked away. The silence answered her question.
"Oh my God!" Lorna said, her voice a whisper. "Tell me it's not true! What did you do to her?"
But still this strange boy, whom yesterday she thought she had fallen in love with, failed to speak. She continued to stare at him, her thoughts racing through her mind. That mysterious boy she met last night wasn't just mysterious. He was weird. What was he? Some kind of pervert? What the hell did he do to Katie?!
She didn't want to find out. Warren's presence suddenly became too much to handle – her emotions were running riot, and she was scared of what he might say next. She had to get out of there. She pushed back her chair.
"Leave me alone! And stay away from my sister!" she shouted.
Turning away, she heard Warren begging her to stay.
"Let me explain! I just want to help!"
But Lorna didn't answer. She just ran out of the canteen without looking back.

Warren's despair grew stronger and stronger, filling his chest until he could hardly breathe. Everything had gone wrong. He hadn't

found the words or the courage to tell Lorna the whole truth, but he had said enough to frighten and shock this beautiful girl.
And the blood! The scent had enveloped him before he had even entered the building. He had chosen a table as near to the kitchen as possible to try and escape the smell. But it was useless. He could not keep the scent of blood away.
The situation had become especially unbearable when Lorna was sitting in front of him. Here, her powerful scent was almost **irresistible**. In the club, he had been able to enjoy the scent while staying in control. In the hospital, however, Warren had needed every last bit of self-discipline to hide his ugly hunger.
And now Lorna was gone. What the hell was he supposed to do now? Warren stood up and walked quickly out of the hospital building. The smell of blood began to fade and Warren sighed with relief. It was a cloudy day, but still Warren **deliberately** headed for the shade. Then he raced back to his little flat as fast as he could.

irresistible	unwiderstehlich
deliberately	mit Absicht
to spin	*hier:* sich drehen
to thump	hämmern

Übung 15: Synonyms. Ordnen Sie jeweils die Synonyme zu!

1. ☐ cry — a) dangerous
2. ☐ weird — b) race
3. ☐ hurry — c) sob
4. ☐ reckless — d) strange

Tears began to trickle down Lorna's cheeks. Her head was **spinning** and her heart was **thumping**. What had Warren done? And where was she supposed to go now? Mum and dad can't see me in this state, she thought. But I can't turn round, not with Warren still in the canteen.

With no real idea where she was going, her feet led her through a series of corridors to the back car park. There, she hoped to be on her own.

elderly	älter
wheelchair	Rollstuhl
covered	*hier:* überdacht
⚡ messed up	verkorkst
to shift	*hier:* sich (von der Stelle) bewegen
to tear sb. apart	*hier:* jmd. das Herz brechen
to curse under one's breath	unterdrückt fluchen

She pushed open a heavy glass door. In the car park a young woman was helping an **elderly** man into a **wheelchair** and a couple of people were parking their cars, but apart from that there was nobody in sight. Lorna sat down on a little wall and put her head in her hands. She began to breathe in and out very slowly and deeply as she tried to control her tears.

"Lorna!" came a voice from behind her. She didn't have to turn her head because she recognized the voice. Ian! Typical! she said to herself. I thought he'd have gone back inside by now!

He was standing about ten metres away from the door in a **covered** area which had SMOKING PERMITTED painted on the ground in big yellow letters. He had a cigarette in one hand and his mobile phone in the other.

"Hi Ian, sorry… Just leave me alone, please. I need some space."

"What's the matter?"

"What do you think? Katie might die! Everything's **messed up**!"

Lorna was trying to breathe slowly, but it was impossible to fully hold back her tears.

Ian walked over to her, sat on the wall and put his hand on her arm.

"Please, just leave me alone!" Lorna said.

She didn't feel comfortable with him so close to her, so she **shifted** along the wall a little, moving away from him.

"Lorna, we're all finding it hard after Katie's accident, but…" Ian began.

Lorna interrupted him with a short laugh, and before she could stop herself she exclaimed, "Huh! Who said it was an accident?!"

"What?" Ian asked. "It wasn't an accident? What do you mean?"
Lorna's emotions were **tearing her apart** – confused and angry, she felt she had to talk to somebody.
"I don't know, Ian! I just don't know."
"What are you saying, Lorna? Do you think somebody *did* this to Katie? Is that what you're saying?"
This time it was Lorna who was silent, apart from her quiet sobbing. Pull yourself together! she told herself, quickly realizing that if Ian knew about Warren, things would be ten times worse. There was no way she could tell Ian. Not with his violent personality! That would never help the situation, would it?
"What do you know?" Ian demanded. "Tell me!"
Still Lorna was quiet. Ian **cursed under his breath** and then threw down his cigarette in anger.
"If I find out that somebody did this to my Katie, then I'll KILL HIM! Do you hear me, Lorna? I'll KILL HIM!"

Übung 16: Answer the questions. Beantworten Sie die Fragen zum Text in ganzen Sätzen!

1. What did Warren feel after Lorna left the canteen?

____

2. Where was Ian permitted to smoke?

____

3. Why was Lorna scared to tell Ian the truth?

____

3 Hypnotized and Horrified

Heavy grey clouds hung over Blackpool and a bitter cold wind was blowing. A few couples and young families were walking up and down the promenade, wrapped up well in their winter coats, hats and scarves. At the tram stop across the road, two old ladies were waiting with their shopping bags, and a teenage girl was trying unsuccessfully to entertain her screaming toddler with a picture book and a teddy bear. In the distance were the bright lights and loud music of Blackpool's North Pier. The pier was practically empty, or at least it appeared so from where Lorna was sitting in the small seaside café. She could see only half a dozen or so tourists, bravely walking out to the pier's Carousel Bar a few hundred metres from the beach, above the Irish Sea.

wrapped up well	warm eingepackt
toddler	Kleinkind
bravely	mutig
forthcoming	bevorstehend
lecture	Vorlesung
rumour	Gerücht
to take one's mind off sth.	sich ablenken

It was a dull, late Monday afternoon. After spending most of the day at Katie's bedside in the hospital, Lorna had come to the café with her books and course notes to study for her forthcoming marketing exam. Lorna was glad not to have any lectures that day, because there was no way she could face the questions and curiosity of the other students – rumours had almost certainly already broken out about Katie's accident. Lorna planned to go back to the hospital later, but just for a short while, she was desperate to escape the depressing atmosphere which filled the hospital and to take her mind off

Katie's condition. Usually she could get lost in her books with no effort at all, but today it seemed impossible. The more she tried to push thoughts about Katie's accident, three nights earlier, to the back of her mind, the more the thoughts seemed to **taunt** her.
The words on the page seemed to jump about from one side to the other, and by the time she finished each paragraph she had already forgotten what she had just read. Repeatedly she found her eyes slowly wandering from the text in front of her to the scene outside the window.
There was little change in Katie's condition. She was still in a coma, **wired up** to the life support machine. The doctors insisted that they were doing everything they could for Katie. All that anybody could really do was wait. Nobody had any answers and that, for Lorna, was the most frustrating thing of all.
But this wasn't completely true. There was one person who did know something, somebody who might have some sort of answer, even if it was unpleasant to hear. Warren.
Back in the canteen on Saturday morning, Lorna's emotions had been **all over the place**. She had felt confused, horrified and **vulnerable** – all at the same time. And she had simply wanted to escape and be on her own.

to taunt	quälen
to be wired up	an etw. angeschlossen sein
↯ all over the place	*hier:* durcheinander
vulnerable	verwundbar

But now Lorna was beginning to regret running away. Watching an old-fashioned tram arrive at the stop to pick up the handful of passengers, Lorna thought about Warren's words: 'Maybe I can help'. What did he know about Katie's accident? Looking back, Lorna was beginning to doubt that this strange and mysterious boy could have hurt her sister. She remembered his behaviour back at the club... his kind words, his gentle kiss... Surely that wasn't just a facade, was it?
And that was why she didn't want to tell Ian anything else about Warren. She re-read a text message Ian had sent her earlier:

Lorna i know ur hiding smt from me - dont deny it. i wanna talk. dont try 2 bullshit me. i'll ring u l8r. ian

Übung 17: Text messaging. Schreiben Sie Ians SMS in korrektem Englisch auf!

___

___

___

It was quite an aggressive text message, and Lorna feared that Ian's actions would be even more violent than his words. Violence wouldn't solve anything, especially when Warren might really have some sort of explanation.

Lorna closed her book and drank the rest of her coffee, which was now cold. It was time to find out what answers Warren really had to offer. She began to write a text message, then deleted the words and tried again. But still the words seemed wrong. Eventually Lorna searched for Warren's phone number and pressed 'dial'.

"Lorna, hi," answered a voice at the other end, after a few seconds. Warren sounded tired, as if the call had woken him up.

"Hello," Lorna said.

She hesitated, but then decided there was no time for small talk, so she got to the point of her call.

"Listen, Warren, I need some answers. Are you free in about an hour?"

to deny	*hier:* abstreiten
ϟ to bullshit sb.	jmd. Scheiß erzählen
to zip up	den Reißverschluss zumachen
to jingle	klimpern
counter	*hier:* Theke
guardian angel	Schutzengel
terraced house	Reihenhaus

"Yes," Warren replied immediately.
"Well, I'll be at the hospital, seeing Katie. She's still asleep. So we could meet at the little café across the road, 'The Full Muffin'. Is that okay?"
"Yes, that's fine," Warren answered. "So at about half past five?"
"Yeah, half past five."
"Thank you for ringing, Lorna. I'm glad you called."
"See you in an hour," said Lorna. Then she hung up, put her book in her bag and **zipped up** her thick winter coat. She got the keys for her little blue car out of her bag, which was full of useful – and useless – bits and pieces, then swung the bag over her shoulder and pulled open the door, causing a little bell above her head to **jingle**. "See you later, love," said the lady behind the **counter**, but Lorna didn't hear her. She was too lost in her own thoughts, already out of the door, walking along the grey, windy Blackpool seafront.

Übung 18: **Prepositions. Lesen Sie weiter und ergänzen Sie, wenn nötig, die fehlenden Präpositionen!**

at | of | outside | - | to | with

Before going back **1.** ______ the hospital, Lorna decided to drive **2.** ______ home and pick up Katie's talisman, a little angel which Katie called her **guardian angel**. She had forgotten to bring it to her sister over the weekend. **3.** ______ about 4:45 p.m. she parked **4.** ______ the little **terraced house** which she rented, along **5.** ______ Katie, Ian and two **6.** ______ Katie's coursemates, Farai and Charlotte.

She locked her car and opened the old front door to their house with her key.
"Hello!" she called as she stepped in.

to squeeze	drücken
to hum	*hier:* summen
accidentally	versehentlich
ϟ to mess with sb.	jmd. zum Narren halten
to feel sick	jmd. wird schlecht
proposal	Vorschlag
be exposed to sb./sth.	jmd./etw. ausgesetzt sein
temper	Laune, Charakter
to set off	losfahren, losgehen

"Hello Lorna!" came a cry from upstairs. It was Farai. Within a few seconds, he came dashing down the stairs.
"Any news from the hospital?" he asked, with a concerned look on his face.
Lorna shook her head. "No. Nothing. I'm heading back now. I just wanted to pick up Katie's guardian angel. She takes it with her wherever she goes."
Farai reached out his hand and **squeezed** Lorna on the arm. "You know we're here if you want to..."
"Yeah, I know I can always come to you, Farai. Thanks," Lorna said, then added, "Have you seen Ian? He said he would phone me, but I've not heard from him."
Farai hesitated. "He, er... he went out to meet Smithy."
"Where?"
Farai hesitated again. "Er... Robinski's Bar, I think."
"Ian's at the pub!" Lorna cried. "I can't believe it! He's out drinking while Katie's in a coma!"
Although she was genuinely annoyed at Ian's apparent lack of concern for Katie, she was also quite relieved – she might be able to avoid a difficult conversation with him if he stayed with Smithy the whole evening.
"Oh well, I suppose I can't stop him. Okay, I'd better get the angel and go."
Lorna headed upstairs and went into Ian and Katie's bedroom to look for the little guardian angel figure. It was on her desk, behind

Ian's open laptop, a pile of books and a collection of dirty mugs and empty beercans. The computer was humming and its screen saver – the words "Ian iz da best" – danced around the screen. Lorna moved the laptop to one side to get to the little angel, and accidentally touched the mousepad. The screensaver disappeared and there, on the screen, appeared an e-mail to Ian from Smithy. Lorna was unable to resist temptation, and began to read the message:

> Hey Mate,
>
> Hope you're OK. We should go for a beer or two to chill out. It'll be good for you. You need to relax.
> So Lorna still isn't telling you anything? It's weird, mate. But if you really heard her say it might not have been an accident, you need to find out what she meant. Get her to speak, then we can find the evil bastard, whoever he is, and tear him to pieces. I will personally help you. WE'LL SHOW HIM NOT TO **MESS WITH** US AGAIN!!
> Anyway, do you wanna meet at 4 in Robinski's? I'll text you in case you don't read this. See you in a bit man,
>
> Smithy

Lorna felt sick. Smithy's e-mail was no joke. The tone of his proposal was angry and violent, and worst of all, it was one hundred percent genuine. He meant what he said. Now her instinct to protect Warren was greater than ever. Whatever he had done, she was sure he didn't deserve to be exposed to Ian and Smithy's violent, thuggish tempers.

If Ian forced her to break her silence, she would just have to lie[i]. Yes, she would insist that Ian had misunderstood her. She had just been upset, that was all, and said things that she didn't mean.

Now, though, she had to take the little guardian angel figure to Katie's bedside. She dashed down the stairs, said goodbye to Farai, jumped into her car and set off for the hospital.

Achtung, Verwechslungsgefahr:

to lie (lay, lain) = liegen
to lie (lied, lied) = lügen

Übung 19: True or false? Welche Aussagen sind korrekt? Kreuzen Sie an!

1. Farai told Lorna there was no news from the hospital. ❒
2. Lorna did not want to tell Ian the truth. ❒
3. Lorna wanted to protect Warren from Ian and Smithy. ❒
4. Smithy offered to help Ian find Katie's attacker. ❒

At 5:20 Warren was waiting in The Full Muffin, a small glass of orange juice in front of him. The little **bulb** hanging from the ceiling seemed to be **struggling** to give off any light at all, but he had sat in the **dimmest** corner of the café anyway. Team photographs of Blackpool Football Club from the past decade hung in a couple of rows on the wall, and an orange and black scarf was hanging over the menu board. Little pots of salt and pepper were on each of the small tables. Warren caught a **whiff** of cooked bacon and sausages which still **lingered** in the air from the breakfast service that morning.

Now, however, the café was only half an hour from closing, and Warren was the only customer there. A young girl had served him his drink, and now she had gone into the kitchen to start cleaning and to **chat** to her friend on her mobile phone.

bulb	Glühbirne
to struggle	*hier:* Mühe haben
dim	dämmrig, düster
whiff	Duft(hauch)
to linger	zurückbleiben, sich halten
to chat	plaudern
out of habit	gewohnheitsmäßig
to distract	ablenken

Warren listened to their conversation, partly **out of habit**, and partly to **distract** himself from his nervousness about seeing Lorna again. The girl in the kitchen had no way of knowing that he could easily hear both sides of the conversation.

"Just decide where you want to go and I'll meet you there," the girl said, bringing the conversation to an end.
"Okay, we'll meet at Tokyo Club at 10 then," came the boy's voice at the other end.
"Right, that's decided," the girl replied. "See you there. Bye!"

to fit in	sich anpassen
suspicion	Verdacht
attentively	aufmerksam
to quiz	ausfragen
moving	rührend, ergreifend

Warren glanced at his watch. It was 17:26. Not long until she arrives now, he thought to himself. He was so nervous he could hardly sit still. He drummed his fingers on the table and tapped his right foot up and down as he waited. He stared at the practically full glass of orange juice in front of him. He wasn't enjoying his drink, but of course he had to buy something. As always, he had to find ways to **fit in**, to look normal. Sometimes Warren felt as if his whole existence was about that and nothing else: fitting in and looking normal. Avoiding **suspicion**. Keeping his head down. Going unnoticed.
Luckily, however, Warren had had a lot of practice at going unnoticed over the years.

Avoiding suspicion was something the Midnight Hunters taught you well, said a voice inside his head. Warren immediately cursed himself. He couldn't be distracted by such thoughts today.
At least over the weekend he had been able to block temptation from his mind and secretly come in and out of the hospital. Nobody had noticed him sitting in a waiting room just a few metres from the intensive care, listening **attentively** to numerous private conversations between the members of Katie's family. He had also heard Katie's macho boyfriend **quiz** Lorna about anything that Lorna might be hiding from him, and was relieved to hear Lorna quickly change the subject. And, each evening, he had heard Lorna share her secrets with her silent sister in **moving** monologues.

"Please don't leave me, Katie," Lorna had begged her sister.
As Warren listened intensely from his seat in a corridor on the other side of the wall to Katie's room, he swallowed.
"I'm your Twinny, remember? You can't leave me!"
Although she had been whispering, Warren could, with some extra effort, hear every last word.
"And I'm sorry for lying to Ian," she had continued, "but I think that boy, Warren, has a good heart. I don't know what exactly he has done, but I'm sure that he didn't mean to **harm** you. I love you so much, Twinny. Please don't leave me."

Übung 20: Word search. Finden Sie in diesem Gitternetz acht Dinge, die im Full Muffin Café zu finden sind!

S	A	T	H	P	P	E	P	P	E	R
Z	A	G	L	E	H	B	L	I	Z	S
K	I	P	R	A	O	L	C	U	O	C
M	B	O	B	X	T	S	T	R	O	A
M	E	N	U	B	O	A	R	D	K	R
B	L	A	L	C	O	L	V	N	Q	F
E	T	A	B	L	E	T	M	L	J	L
O	R	A	N	G	E	J	U	I	C	E

1. ____________________ 5. ____________________

2. ____________________ 6. ____________________

3. ____________________ 7. ____________________

4. ____________________ 8. ____________________

At exactly 5:30, Warren heard the sound of the café door opening and looked up to see Lorna entering. She was wearing a thick coat and carrying a large bag. Warren tried to make eye contact with her, but she simply walked over to the counter, called for the young girl, ordered and paid for a can of lemonade. Then finally, with the drink in one hand and her purse in the other, she headed over to the table in the dimly lit corner.

Then, their eyes met for the first time since their **encounter** in the hospital canteen. Warren tried to read Lorna's eyes, but her expression seemed quite neutral. What was she thinking? Was she angry? Nervous? Afraid? He wasn't sure. Maybe, he thought, she's trying to **keep her cards close to her chest**. I don't **blame** her if she is, he thought. Lorna placed the can and her purse on the table and dropped her large bag on the floor. Dressed in a **baggy** jumper, jeans and trainers, and with her hair tied back in a messy ponytail, she looked far from elegant. After days in the hospital, Warren had secretly seen how the stress and worry was **taking its toll on** her, but this didn't bother him in the slightest. Lorna's real beauty had lost nothing. Her eyes still shone like bright stars and her body still gave off that intoxicating, overwhelming scent. And despite everything, Warren couldn't help but be excited by this.

"Thank you for coming to meet me," she said in a voice that sounded quite distant and impersonal. She **was** clearly **on her guard**. She sounded exhausted, too, but this was no surprise to Warren, who knew exactly how little she had slept the whole weekend long.

to harm sb.	jmd. schaden, jmd. verletzen
encounter	Begegnung
to keep one's cards close to one's chest	sich nicht in die Karten schauen lassen, sich bedeckt halten
to blame sb.	jmd. etw. übel nehmen
baggy	schlabberig
to take its toll on	Auswirkungen haben, seinen Tribut fordern von
to be on one's guard	auf der Hut sein

"Thank *you* for calling me," Warren answered. "I'm glad you changed your mind."
"I just want to know what exactly happened to Katie in the club."
"I want to tell you everything, Lorna. I really do. But you have to give me a chance, and that won't be easy."
"Just tell me the truth, then. Who are you?"
"I am the boy you met on Friday night. That was the real me, I promise. But I'm not *just* that boy... That's just one side of me."

fairytale	Märchen
firm	*hier:* entschieden
to falter	stocken
to emphasize	betonen
coffin	Sarg
vicious	bösartig

Lorna opened her mouth as if she was about to speak, but then just sighed. Warren took this as a sign to continue.
"I have hopes and dreams, emotions and fears, just like you and just like Katie. We're not that [i] different. Except..." Warren sighed. "Except I'm not really... human."
"I'm sorry," Lorna said with a confused and frustrated expression on her face, "but I don't have time for this, Warren. You said you could help me. I wanted some real answers, not a fairytale."
"Okay, Lorna," Warren said, desperate to keep her calm.
The more he talked, the more frustrated Lorna became. He realized that talking around the truth was not helping – he just had to get to the point and say the word. Warren leant forward in his chair and looked Lorna straight in the eye. Then he spoke. He lowered his voice, but he kept it firm and did not falter.
"The truth is, Lorna, I'm not human. The truth is, I'm a vampire."

That kann einem Adjektiv vorangestellt werden und dient dann der Verstärkung:

We're not **that** different.
= Wir sind gar nicht so unterschiedlich.

Is he really **that** busy?
= Ist er wirklich so beschäftigt?

Übung 21: Word forms. Ergänzen Sie das jeweilige Substantiv und Adverb!

1. suspicious __________ __________
2. neutral __________ __________
3. angry __________ __________
4. emotional __________ __________

For a second, Lorna's brain didn't take in what he had just said – the word 'vampire'. Then the absurdity of the situation hit her. This handsome, kind-hearted and intelligent boy was actually mad!

"A vampire," Lorna said, swallowing hard. "Good God, I knew you were going to shock me, but... wow! Warren, are you... are you actually crazy? I mean, do you take some kind of medication?"

"No, no! Just listen. You need to give me a chance to explain."

Explain? Lorna thought to herself. Explain?! He tells me that he's a supernatural creature and then thinks it's something he can explain! But she had come here demanding the truth. And if she wanted it, she had to be patient. She had to give him a chance.

She sighed. "What do you mean, 'vampire'? I don't understand what you're trying to tell me. I mean, vampires don't *exist*, do they? And what does this have to do with Katie?"

"The thing is," Warren said, speaking slowly and emphasizing each word, "vampires *do* exist. We don't sleep in coffins and we don't wear big black capes, but we're real. Many vampires are evil – they just act on instinct... vicious creatures with no sense of right and wrong and no concept of the value of human life. But I'm not like that. I know about that kind of existence all too well, but I hate everything about it. I try and live just like everybody else – like humans."

Although Warren's story was surely nothing but madness, Lorna felt uneasy, just as she had in the canteen. There was something about the way he told it – perhaps it was Warren's hypnotizing stare – that made this fantastic story sound as if it might almost be true. She sat bolt upright in her chair, her arms crossed tightly across her stomach.

Übung 22: Translation. Lesen Sie weiter und übersetzen Sie die markierten Wörter!

"Just like other vampires, I have highly developed **1.** Sinne ___________ – sight, hearing, **2.** Geruch ___________... and I can move much faster than any human on earth, too. I suppose you could say these are **3.** etwas ___________ like my special powers. But then there's the other **4.** Seite ___________. Just like other vampires, I still have to feed to live, if you can call my existence living. I need blood. There's no question about it – I need it. And that," Warren said, **5.** langsam ___________ and quietly, "is where Katie's accident comes into the **6.** Geschichte ___________."

Lorna's heart began to beat faster. Making a connection to Katie made Warren's story so much more worrying. Blood? Katie?! Lorna's heart beat faster still.
She started to notice things about Warren which she hadn't noticed before. His skin was very pale and unblemished – no scars, spots or imperfections. And his eyes... those eyes! Like laser beams! Lorna

pale	blass
unblemished	makellos
scar	Narbe
laser beam	Laserstrahl
to grip	ergreifen, erfassen
contradictory	widersprüchlich
to seduce	verführen
surroundings *pl*	Umgebung
goose pimples *pl*	Gänsehaut

felt Warren's stare burning on her face. She suddenly realized that his whole beauty was connected to some overwhelming power. Lorna was gripped by bizarre, contradictory feelings – Warren's power both seduced and terrified her.

Run away! her instinct told her. Run now, while you still can!

The situation was so much more intense than it had been back in the cafeteria. Her surroundings seemed to have disappeared into insignificance. Her head told her to leave but still she couldn't move. Her body was covered in goose pimples, but not from fear, she realized. No, she felt strangely excited.

"When I met you in the club, I knew that you were special, Lorna. I knew that you were different to every other girl there. Hell, I knew you were different to every other girl in Blackpool. You had this... aura. I wanted so badly to be with you. Then, at the bar, I saw Katie, and I thought it was you. I tried to talk to her, but she pushed me away. There was a boy with her, too, and... God, Lorna, I was so hurt and confused."

Hurt and confused? This sounded almost ridiculous to Lorna. How could this boy... no, this creature, here in front of her... how could someone so powerful ever feel hurt or confused? But Lorna did not laugh. She couldn't move a muscle. She was completely spellbound.

Warren continued. "'How could Lorna do this to me?' I asked myself. But of course it wasn't you. It was Katie. And then when she cut her hand, my hunger for blood became uncontrollable. My confusion had turned to anger, and so I followed Katie to the toilets and ... I fed on her."

Panic gripped Lorna's entire body, but still, she couldn't move. Warren's presence had taken away any control that she once had.

She felt as if he were holding her down without even touching her. This fascinating boy... was also fascinated by me?! And then he drank Katie's blood?! Conflicting emotions raced through her head – lust and repulsion, sympathy and anger.
"Lorna, I'm sorry this is hard to hear," Warren continued, and started to reach his hand across the table, "but you have to..."
Suddenly, Lorna **regained** control of her body and her instinct to escape sprang into action.

Übung 23: **Infinitive or present participle? Lesen Sie weiter und unterstreichen Sie die richtige Variante!**

"Don't **1.** touch / touching me!" she cried, **leaping** back from the table as she **flung** out her arm to push Warren's hand away from her. At the same time, she also managed to **2.** hit / hitting her unopened can of lemonade and send it **3.** fly / flying off the table.
Then, as Lorna sat helplessly **4.** watch / watching the can spinning through the air, something extraordinary happened. Within a split second, a blurred object flashed from Warren's chair to the can – some metres from the table – and then back to where Warren had been **5.** sit / sitting. And right in front of her disbelieving eyes, Lorna watched as the **blurred** object turned back into Warren sitting on his chair and **6.** hold / holding the can of lemonade.

to regain	wieder-gewinnen
to leap	einen Satz machen
to fling	schleudern
blurred	verschwommen
disbelief	Fassungs-losigkeit
to burst into tears	in Tränen ausbrechen

Lorna's mouth fell open in pure shock. But deep inside, her disbelief began to disappear. This was proof that Warren was not crazy. The horrible truth was becoming ever clearer: Everything he had said was true.

Warren placed the can to one side.

"I was responsible for what happened to Katie," he continued. "But I am so very sorry, and now I just want to... to try and put things right. But if she's going to... If Katie's not going to wake up, I need to know. Because I could save her, by making her like... like me."

Lorna's head spun faster than ever. Just when she thought things couldn't get any crazier, Warren was proposing to turn her sister into a vampire?! That was really too much. Emotion overwhelmed her, and all Lorna could do was to burst into tears. She closed her eyes and put her face in her hands. She felt her heart thumping and once again she felt panic and fear. Again, her instinct was to run away, to escape the creature in front of her.

She opened her eyes. Warren was still sitting in front of her. His face was more neutral now, but his hand reached out over the table. Lorna knew it was a gesture of comfort, but there was no way she could accept it.

"You drank my sister's blood," she finally managed to say. "And now you want to make her like you! Well, if that is your idea [i] of a solution, Warren, then I don't want to hear it..."

Idea heißt sowohl „Idee" als auch „Vorstellung" oder „Ahnung":

to have an idea
= eine Idee haben

to have an idea of sth.
= eine Vorstellung von etw. haben

to have no idea
= keine Ahnung haben

Übung 24: Negating prefixes. Ordnen Sie jedem Adjektiv die entsprechende Vorsilbe zu!

1. ☐	dis-	a) responsible
2. ☐	ir-	b) belief
3. ☐	un-	c) significance
4. ☐	in-	d) believable

The sound of her phone vibrating interrupted her. Lorna stopped talking and started looking for it in her bag.

"It's my dad," she said when she had finally found it.

She took a deep breath.

"Hello? Dad?" Her voice was still quite **choked** from her sobbing.

"Lorna?" came her father's voice at the other end.

Lorna was filled with anxiety. Was the call bad news?

"Yes, Dad. What is it?"

"Lorna, it's Katie! She's awake! She's awake!"

"What?" Lorna was once again so shocked she could not speak.

"Come to the hospital, Lorna. You've got to..."

"Katie's awake? Yeah, Dad, of course. I'll be... Are you sure? Is everything okay? Is she really..."

"Yes! She's back, Lorna. She's awake!"

"Okay, Dad, I'm on my way!"

"Come right away, Sweetheart. I love you."

"I love you, too, Dad," Lorna said, holding back her tears, and then the *click* at the other end signalled that her father had hung up.

Lorna turned to Warren.

choked	krächzend
cloth	Lappen
astonishment	Verwunderung
sincerity	Aufrichtigkeit

"Katie's awake," she said quietly, and then repeated the words, this time crying out with joy. "Katie has woken up!"
"Is everything okay?" asked the young girl who worked in the café.
Lorna glanced over to see that she was standing behind the counter with a cloth in one hand and disinfectant in the other. She had a look of astonishment on her face.
"Everything's fine!" Warren called over to her and then turned back to Lorna. "I'm so, so happy for you, Lorna."
"Oh my God!" Lorna exclaimed. "I was so worried that... I was so, so worried that she'd never..."
"Well, it doesn't matter now. You should go to the hospital."
"Yeah, I've got to go. I've got to see Katie." She quickly picked up her bag and purse, then turned to Warren, who was still seated.
"You'll never understand just how sorry I am, Lorna," Warren said to her. "I mean that."
Lorna couldn't help but notice the sincerity in his voice. But there was nothing that she could say in reply. She turned away, thanked the girl and stepped out into the street. Then she hurried towards the hospital entrance, desperate to see her sister.

The sun had set by now and there was only a dim light from the streetlights, but Warren, of course, had no problem watching Lorna cross the road and head towards the hospital entrance.
"I'm sorry about that," Warren said to the young girl. "We just had some really good news."
"Oh, that's okay," the girl replied. "I'm happy for you."
"Thanks," Warren said, and walked towards the door, leaving a full glass and an unopened can on the table.
"Doing anything nice tonight?" the girl asked in a friendly voice, before Warren had a chance to leave.
Warren tried quickly to think of a polite but short answer.
"Erm, no, not really."

He opened the door. Then he looked back at the girl and smiled, his happiness shining through.
"Have a great evening at Tokyo Club!" he winked as he left the café, leaving her staring after him in astonishment.

Übung 25: Indirect speech. Wer hat was gesagt? Ergänzen Sie die fehlenden Personen!

Lorna | Mr Irvine | The girl in the café | Warren

1. ________ asked Warren if he was doing anything nice that evening.
2. ________ told Lorna that she would never understand how sorry he was.
3. ________ told Lorna to come to the hospital straight away.
4. ________ said that Katie had woken up.

4 Midnight Hunters

"Any questions?" the lecturer asked.

Lorna wondered if 'Would you mind explaining all of the theories of tourism sociology all over again, Dr Rostock?' was an acceptable question. However, Lorna would never have dared to ask the lecturer this question, not even as a joke. Dr Rostock was one of the less conventional lecturers in the Travel and Tourism department. She had a huge serpent tattoo on her arm and a shaven head. She had no time for lazy students and was known for her scathing remarks and bad temper. This was not a woman Lorna – or anyone else, in fact – wanted to cross.

So nobody raised their hand to ask a question or interrupted the silence.

"Okay then, if nobody has any questions, then all I shall say is good luck with your essays. I'm expecting good things."

This brought the lecture to a close. Lorna had only had two lectures that day, so she had taken the opportunity to spend the morning and early afternoon at her parents' house with her sister, before coming into university to catch up with some studying and attend her two lectures. It was four days since Katie had woken up, and Lorna was just starting to feel comfortable with her university work again. Katie had arrived at her parents' house from the hospital the previous day. Mrs Irvine had insisted that she stayed there, where she could take good care of her, until she was fully better.

lecturer	Dozent(in)
to dare	wagen
serpent	Schlange
scathing	vernichtend
bad temper	üble Laune
to attend	teilnehmen an

"Do you **fancy** coming round to my place tonight to watch some TV?" asked Helena, Lorna's best friend and coursemate.
After a week in bed ill, she was now fully recovered and back at university. Now the two girls were packing away their files and books.
"Unless you're planning to see Katie?"
"I spent time with Katie earlier, so yeah, that sounds great," Lorna answered. "It's been **ages** since we chilled out together."

Übung 26: Idiomatic expressions. Schreiben Sie die Sätze neu und verwenden Sie dabei die folgenden Begriffe!

cards | fancy | toll | ages

1. "How lovely to see you again! **It's been such a very long time** since we last met." ______________________

____

2. The stress **is really having a negative affect on her health.** ______________________

____

3. He asks lots of questions but **tells me very little about what he is really thinking.** ______________________

____

4. **Would you like to go dancing** in that new club tonight?

____

____

The two girls walked out into the dark and towards the street where Lorna's little car was parked. There was so much Lorna wanted to share with Helena – secrets that she had kept to herself. But how could she start to explain everything? Although she could trust her best friend, it seemed dangerous even to mention the name of her mysterious new **acquaintance**. And how could she tell Helena when she hadn't even told Katie?

ϟ to fancy doing sth.	Lust haben, etw. zu tun
ages	eine Ewigkeit
acquaintance	Bekanntschaft
to fasten one's seatbelt	sich anschnallen
headlight	Scheinwerfer
hesitancy	Unschlüssigkeit

"So," Helena said when they had reached the car and got inside, "how is Katie? I mean, she must still be pretty weak, right?"
"Yes," Lorna replied, "she's still quite weak. To be honest, on Monday when she woke up, I thought that would be the end of it. I thought she'd be fine and able to come home straight away."
"No, I think it takes a while, Lorna. Like you said before, at first she could only stay awake for half an hour each time. It's not like in the films when people just wake up and then get on with their lives[i]."
"Yeah, I suppose so," Lorna sighed.

She put her bag on the backseat and **fastened her seatbelt**, then started the car's engine and turned the **headlights** on.

Die Pluralform von Substantiven, die auf -f oder -fe enden, wird im Englischen oft mit -ves gebildet, z. B.:

life – lives	half – halves
wife – wives	shelf – shelves

"You know, there's something else I wanted to mention," Helena said.
Lorna heard the **hesitancy** in her friend's voice.
"Yeah, Hel? What is it?" Lorna asked, slightly concerned.
She pulled the car out of the parking space and set off down the street.
"I saw Ian earlier. Just before Dr Rostock's lecture," Helena replied.
"Ian? What was he doing on campus?"

Übung 27: Indefinite pronouns. Lesen Sie weiter und setzen Sie die korrekten Indefinitpronomen ein!

anything | nothing | somebody | something | something

"I'm not sure. It was a bit weird. I was walking towards the east block when I saw you about fifty metres ahead. I was going to catch you up, but then I noticed **1.** ________ in the east car park hiding behind a van, looking in your direction. At first I thought **2.** ________ of it. Then I got closer and the man turned towards me; it was Ian."

"Really? So did he see you? Did you speak to him?"

"Yeah, he realized I had seen him straight away. I just said 'Hi, Ian'. I didn't say **3.** ________ else. But he immediately got very defensive. He said **4.** ________ like 'I was just looking for a friend', even though I hadn't asked him what he was doing there. He seemed very annoyed that I had seen him. And then he did **5.** ________ really weird."

Lorna began to worry. What could Ian have done? This was obviously connected to his suspicions that she was hiding something. Had Ian started **spying on** her?

"What is it?" Lorna asked, impatiently. "What did he do?"

"He got really, really worked up. I thought he was going to become violent! He was starting to scare me a bit when he walked over to me, grabbed my arm and said: 'What has Lorna told you? What do you know?' I said I didn't know what he was talking about, but he wasn't listening. He said something like 'Who hurt Katie? What is Lorna hiding from me?' I know it sounds stupid, but I was scared, Lorna. I thought he was going to hit me. Then he calmed down and looked a bit embarrassed. I just wanted to get out of there."

"What on earth does Ian think he's doing? I can't believe it! Are you okay now, Hel?" asked Lorna, deeply concerned.

"Yeah, yeah, I'm fine. Though to be honest I did feel really intimidated. He told me not to tell you. In fact, he threatened me. But of course I wanted to tell you. I can't believe you have to live with such a thug!"

"God, I know," Lorna said, sighing. She had been living with Ian for only two months – it had been supposed to be a temporary arrangement – but it was two months too long.

"So what happened then?"

"Well, I think he suddenly realized how inappropriate his behaviour was, so he let go of my arm and stormed off. I was so shocked, I just stood there for a minute, unable to believe what had happened. I'm okay now, really. But I'm still a bit confused. What was Ian talking about? I mean, who says somebody hurt Katie? Is there really something you're not telling Ian? You know I'd never tell him."

Lorna felt her conscience being torn in two. Could she really tell Helena? She had no idea what was the right thing to do. Should she

to spy on sb.	jmd. nachspionieren
ϟ to get worked up	sich über etw. aufregen
ϟ What on earth…!	Was zum Teufel…!
to intimidate	einschüchtern
to threaten	drohen
inappropriate	unangemessen
conscience	Gewissen
torn in two	*hier:* zwiegespalten

lie to her best friend? Or should she tell the truth and potentially **endanger** Warren – that mysterious creature to whom she was still strangely attracted. As much as she feared Warren, Lorna could not stop certain thoughts from entering her head – lustful, exciting fantasies about the vampire danced around her confused mind. How could Helena understand her complex and contradictory feelings? And what on earth would she say when Lorna started talking about vampires?! She would surely think her friend had gone completely mad! Then Lorna suddenly had a **brainwave**. Perhaps there was a way of being **faithful** to both Helena and Warren? She began to explain.
"So you promise this stays between you and me?"
"Of course, Lorna. You're my best friend."

to endanger	gefährden
brainwave	Geistesblitz
faithful	treu
sympathy	Mitgefühl
turmoil	Aufruhr

"Well, you see, there's this boy. Warren, he's called."
"A boy?! Lorna, why haven't you told me this before?!"
"Because everything has been so chaotic with Katie's accident. I felt guilty enough just for seeing him. And that's why I couldn't tell Ian. I was scared he would be angry. There have been a couple of times when I've seen Warren, and I've had to lie to Ian about where I've been. So he knows I'm hiding something. And for some reason, he thinks it is linked to Katie's accident."
Okay, Lorna thought to herself, so I'm playing with the truth a little, but half-truths are not lies, are they?
"Oh, I see. You felt guilty for thinking about him when everybody else was so worried about Katie."
"Exactly."
The more Lorna thought about it, the more she realized this was completely true. She did feel guilty for being attracted to Warren. But to Lorna's surprise, she realized that she was also beginning to feel **sympathy** for Warren's moral **turmoil** – his personal struggle to fight

his bloodthirsty instinct. Could it be that she hated the sin but loved the sinner?

Lorna turned into Helena's street, parked her car and the girls headed into Helena's house. In the kitchen, Helena put the kettle on, took two mugs out of a cupboard and put a teabag in each. Lorna put her car keys and mobile phone in the middle of the kitchen table, and both girls sat down.

"So tell me more! Who is this 'Warren'?!" Helena asked, as she sat down at the kitchen table.

Now this is going to be the trickier part, Lorna thought.

"I met him in the club on Halloween. We got talking and he seemed really nice. We had loads to talk about. We just seemed to click!"

"So when did you speak to him last?"

"Last Monday. The day Katie woke up."

"So long ago? Why haven't you been in contact since?"

Lorna hesitated. "I'm not sure if it'd be the best idea to... I mean, with Ian and everything, it might be complicated."

"Lorna! You can't let Ian run your life! You obviously still like this boy, so ring him! In fact, you should ring him now."

"Now?! Okay, okay. Maybe later."

"Okay, later. But right now you can go and make that tea," Helena said as the kettle finished boiling.

Lorna thought Helena's smile was a little suspicious, but she got up anyway and walked over to the kettle. When she had filled the two mugs with boiling water, she walked back to the table and saw the mischievous grin on Helena's face. What had she done?

Lorna gasped. There, in the middle of the table, was her phone. And on the screen were the words 'Calling WARREN'.

to put the kettle on	Wasser aufsetzen
ϟ to click	sich auf Anhieb verstehen
mischievous	spitzbübisch, verschmitzt
to gasp	nach Luft schnappen

"Helena!" she exclaimed. "You're crazy!"
It was impossible to really be angry wih Helena and she gave a little laugh. At the same time her heart jumped with excitement at the thought of speaking to Warren again. She felt like a teenager again, with hundreds of butterflies suddenly fluttering around in her stomach. She put the phone to her ear and a second later she heard Warren's voice at the other end. "Hello?"
"Hi, erm, Warren," Lorna answered, looking at Helena. Her friend was sitting with a very smug look on her face.

Übung 28: Apostrophes. Lesen Sie weiter und ergänzen Sie bei den markierten Wörtern, falls nötig, den Apostroph!

"Hi, Lorna," Warren answered. "How are you? And **1.** hows ____________ Katie?"

He sounded a little bewildered.

"**2.** Im _______ fine, **3.** thanks ___________. And **4.** Katies _____________ getting better. She left the hospital last night and is staying at my **5.** parents _______________ house."

"Oh, **6.** thats ____________ good news," Warren replied.

A slightly awkward moment of silence followed.
Then Warren spoke again. "I'm really glad you rang."
"Yeah, I just wanted to... I was wondering how you were."
Lorna felt very uncomfortable – not to be talking to Warren, but to have Helena listening.
"Lorna, I'm fine. Still relieved that Katie woke up, and still really..."

"Oh, so is everybody else," Lorna said, interrupting Warren. She wasn't sure how much Helena could hear, but she certainly didn't want Warren to start mentioning his dark secret.
"Maybe we could meet again," Warren suggested. "I mean, if you..."
"Sure," Lorna replied, before she could stop herself. "Sounds great."

smug	süffisant
bewildered	verwirrt
awkward	unangenehm, peinlich
multi-storey car park	Parkhaus
to rush	hetzen, hasten
Cupid	Amor

"Erm, fantastic," Warren replied. He sounded surprised that Lorna had answered so quickly and without hesitation.
"Are you free tonight?"
"Tonight?" Lorna replied, glancing at her friend.
Helena was nodding enthusiastically.
"Yes okay, why not. Where shall we meet?"
"Maybe Wellington road?" Warren suggested. "There's the **multi-storey car park** in the side street, so you don't have to worry about parking. There are quite a few nice bars, too."
"Sounds good," Lorna replied.
Lorna didn't want to sound as if she were **rushing** the conversation, but it was difficult to hide her anxiety. "Okay, I'll see you in... erm..."
"About an hour and a half?" Warren asked.
"Yeah, an hour and a half is fine," Lorna replied.
"Great. I'll see you by the entrance to the car park, or just inside the car park if it starts to rain again. And I'm really sorry..."
Lorna's anxiety took over – she had to end the call before Warren said something that would make Helena suspicious.
"Bye, Warren!" She said and put the phone down.
"This is *fantastic*!" Helena cried out. "I *knew* you wanted to see him. I knew it! Just call me **Cupid**."
"I cannot believe you did that!" Lorna replied, trying once again unsuccessfully to sound annoyed.

"Oh don't pretend you're not grateful!" Helena laughed.
Lorna smiled. "Okay, okay. Thank you, Cupid. Anyway, I'd better get going. I've got to get changed."
"And I shall want to know all the juicy details," Helena said excitedly.
Lorna swallowed hard. If only her friend knew the irony of what she had just said.
Still uncertain, but full of excitement, Lorna said goodbye to Helena, picked up her keys and phone, and headed home to get ready.

Übung 29: Translation. Übersetzen Sie die folgenden Sätze ins Deutsche!

1. The conversation was a little awkward at first.

____

2. I'm relieved that Katie's woken up.

____

3. Let's meet by the entrance to the multi-storey car park.

____

4. Lorna answered without hesitation.

____

An hour later, Lorna was standing in front of her full-length mirror wearing a green dress, a white cardigan and high heels. She wondered if she was overdressed? It was not a date, after all! It was just a drink. Just a drink to talk things over. No, she certainly couldn't date a vampire!

She walked out of her room and went downstairs. She was glad Ian was not there. My God he'd be suspicious if he saw her! If he found out about tonight, she would never be able to explain herself.

to pretend	so tun, als ob
↯ juicy	pikant (wörtlich: saftig)
to gather	sammeln

She was still disturbed by Ian's behaviour towards Helena, and indeed towards herself. Was there really no way of convincing him that it was one huge misunderstanding? That, Lorna thought to herself, is something I'll have to sort out sooner rather than later. But not tonight. Tonight is about Warren, not Ian.

"Bye, Farai!" Lorna shouted.

"See you later," came the reply from her flatmate's bedroom.

Luckily he hadn't seen her either. Just keep things as simple as possible, Lorna told herself.

A minute later she was in her car, heading towards Wellington Road.

It took a while for Warren to really believe he was going to see Lorna again. How was it possible that she wanted to see him again?

He went home and relaxed for a while, trying to **gather** his thoughts and to think rationally. This is an opportunity for a second chance, he told himself. Lorna isn't trying to trick me. She wouldn't do that.

He got changed, choosing a casual shirt and trousers and brown loafers, then he left his flat. He set off towards Wellington Road, a lively street offering some of the classier bars in Blackpool. It was the first night in a few weeks that the autumn night sky was clear, and thousands of stars were shining brightly. Much closer, but still in the distance, Warren could see the famous Blackpool illuminations, the bright lights which lit up the road along the seafront.

Now Warren was walking along a quiet street next to the car park. He could see his planned meeting point with Lorna, just one hundred metres or so away on the other side of the road. He had passed only a few individuals, when suddenly a group of people turned into the street from the other end and began to head in his direction. As he **approached** the group, Warren began to realize who the figures were. At first, it wasn't their faces that Warren recognized but their movements. To the ordinary human eye, it may have looked as if they were walking. Warren, however, saw that they weren't walking – they were **prowling**. There was no doubt about it. The figures were the Midnight Hunters.

Übung 30: Americanisms. Die folgenden Vokabeln sind alle typisch für das amerikanische Englisch. Finden Sie im Text die entsprechenden Synonyme in britischem Englisch!

1. pants ____________________
2. apartment ____________________
3. fall ____________________
4. parking lot ____________________

Instantly, Warren was filled with horror and his instinct was to turn and flee. He had **dreaded** this moment since the phone call with Toby, but he hadn't expected it to come so soon. Although he wasn't scared of the vampires, he **despised** everything about them. He knew that any encounter with them would be **tense** at best, and violent at worst.

But fleeing was **pointless**. The vampires had seen him; Warren could already feel their stare. Warren's basic

to approach	zugehen auf, sich nähern
to prowl	herumstreifen, pirschen
to dread	fürchten, jmd. graut vor
to despise	verachten
tense	angespannt
pointless	sinnlos

instincts took over. He took on an aggressive posture, arching his back slightly like a fierce animal and curling his fingers tightly towards his palms, like claws. He ground his teeth as his whole body became tense.

"Well, what a nice surprise!" came the sarcastic voice of the largest of the six vampires. "Our paths cross again. It's been a long time, Warren." They were just a few metres away.

"I didn't expect to see you out. Isn't it past your bedtime? This place can be dangerous after dark, you know."

The other vampire, too, stood with a very aggressive posture.

"I think I can take care of myself, thank you, Rory," Warren replied sarcastically.

Several centimetres taller than Warren, and extremely well-built, Rory, the ringleader, was an intimidating sight. Warren was perfectly aware of the size of the biceps under Rory's coat sleeves, but still he wasn't afraid. The ringleader's physical strength didn't concern Warren too much, because as strong as Rory was, he wasn't stupid enough to do Warren any lasting harm. The conflict that might break out within the vampire world simply wasn't worth it.

"Yeah, we know," Rory snarled, once again with sarcasm.

His black hair was hard with gel, shaped into several spikes on the top of his head. He was wearing a long leather coat, black jeans and huge black boots. With his gothic attire and black fingernails, Warren thought Rory looked like a caricature of the twenty-first century vampire.

posture	Körperhaltung
to arch	*hier:* spannen
fierce	wild, gefährlich
to curl	sich einrollen
palm	*hier:* Handfläche
to grind one's teeth	mit den Zähnen knirschen
ringleader	Anführer
to be aware of sth.	sich einer Sache bewusst sein
sth.'s not worth it	etw. lohnt sich nicht
to snarl	die Zähne fletschen, knurren
spike	Stachel
attire	Kleidung

"We've seen what little Warren **is capable of**. Impressive, I'll give you that," Rory remarked nonchalantly.
"Am I supposed to know what you're talking about?" Warren asked **through gritted teeth**.
"Let's just say that you weren't the only one hunting on Halloween. I wanted to celebrate my return to Blackpool, so I thought I'd join the party. I'm surprised you didn't notice someone else on your **patch**. Maybe your mind was elsewhere?"
"You were in Visage Club that night?"
"I certainly was, sunshine. I certainly was."
Rory pronounced his words with an unusally fine English accent that didn't go with his **rough** image at all. Warren had once thought that Rory sounded more like an aristocrat than the leader of a vicious, supernatural pack of hunters.
Rory continued. "I saw your fine work. That girl didn't know what had hit her! Of course I quite understand", he said, pretending sympathy. "When blood is served on a plate like that, you've got to take it! But then, the poor, helpless creature taken off in an ambulance! I couldn't believe it. Good, innocent little Warren doing something terrible like that? Moral Warren, always worried about doing the right thing? Surely not him? But surprise surprise – it *was* you! You've certainly changed."
Warren took a step backwards but **maintained** his tense posture.
"You have no idea, Rory," he said. "It wasn't what it seemed."
One of the smaller vampires in the gang gave a sharp laugh. The gang-members stood on either side of their leader, each one with his back arched, like Warren, and ready to **pounce** if necessary.

to be capable of	zu etw. fähig sein
through gritted teeth	mit zusammengebissenen Zähnen
patch	*hier:* Revier
rough	grob
to maintain	(bei)behalten
to pounce	sich auf etw. stürzen

"Oh, I know exactly what it was!" Rory smiled. "Because it was our kind of attack. The attack of a Midnight Hunter. Tell me, are you finally regretting leaving us?"
For the Midnight Hunters, hunting was a sport – a blood sport, so to speak. Hunting was their thrill, their kick, their **high**. And then, the drinking of the victim's blood – that was their ecstasy, their moment of pure **bliss**.
For Warren it had once also been pure bliss, until his **epiphany** – his realization of the pure evil of the gang. And ever since that moment, Warren had carried around with him the shame he felt for his dark past – a burden that never seemed to get any lighter.
"Maybe you're interested in hearing our plans for this fine evening. We're on our way to Granville Road. I hear there'll be a fine selection to feast on there. I'm getting thirsty just thinking about it. I'm sure we'll have **sucked** the life out of the party by the early hours of the morning, if you know what I mean! Don't tell me you're not tempted."
Rory's words created a bitter anger deep inside Warren – anger at Rory, but also at himself for his all too recent Halloween attack.
"Save your breath, Rory. I'm not interested."
"Pardon?" Rory took another step towards Warren.

high	*hier:* Rausch
bliss	Seligkeit
epiphany	Erleuchtung
to suck	saugen
⚡ Jog on!	Hau ab!
to recommend	empfehlen

Warren felt his anger boiling hotter and hotter, deeper and deeper. Keep your cool! he told himself. Don't lose your temper! That won't help. But he couldn't help it – his anger took control of his words.
"I meant you can all get lost. **Jog on!** You know you're..."
"I beg your pardon?" Rory said slowly, icily now, interrupting Warren. "My good man, I do **recommend** you are a little more careful what you say. I hate to have to remind you who I am, and what I might do

if you annoy me, you pathetic little..."
Warren couldn't hold his rage back any longer. It exploded out of his mouth.
"You're repulsive, Rory, you know that? And you're a **coward**! What you do to those girls is a coward's work. But congratulations! This must be the first time you've picked on someone your own size in..."

Übung 31: Correct the mistakes. Lesen Sie weiter und korrigieren Sie die sechs Fehler im folgenden Textabschnitt!

Warren was interrupted, but not by Rory's words. This time it was Rory's fist. Like a flash of lightning, it swinged round from Warrens left. Warren saw it coming, but Rory was to quick for him. Warren's reflexes were fast but Rory's movements were quickly. Warren felt the blow hitted him hard on the left-hand side of his head. He felt himself falling and could see the clapping hands and smiling faces of the other Midnight Hunters. Then the faces become blurred and everything went black.

1. ____________________ 4. ____________________

2. ____________________ 5. ____________________

3. ____________________ 6. ____________________

Lorna's heart was racing. She had seen everything – Warren, the gang, the confrontation, the attack. She had parked her car in the car park and exited into the quiet side street. She had seen the gang walk past on the other side of the road, and then, twenty seconds later, she had

coward	Feigling
to witness	miterleben, Zeuge sein
paralysed	gelähmt
compassion	Mitgefühl
within earshot	in Hörweite
to crouch down	in die Hocke gehen

heard the confrontation. At first she had paid no attention. Only when she heard Warren's name mentioned, Lorna decided to hide behind a series of vehicles, trying to carefully get closer to the scene, where she witnessed the ugly exchange of words. At first she hadn't understood. What were they going to do at Granville Road? What did he mean by 'a fine selection to feast on'? But then to her horror she began to understand exactly what the guy was referring to. Suck away the life from the party?! These were the vicious vampires Warren had warned her about. They were hunters! Blood-hunters!

And then the one who seemed to be the ringleader had punched Warren and sent him flying to the ground. Now, hidden behind a van on the other side of the road and scared for Warren's life and her own, she didn't know what to do. Warren was lying completely motionless on the pavement and the gang were walking away, laughing with one another and congratulating their leader.

Oh Warren! Oh Warren, please be okay! Lorna thought to herself. She wanted so much to go over and help him, but she was paralysed with fear that the gang might turn back and see her.

But suddenly, for one moment her compassion was greater than her fear and Lorna ran to Warren's side as fast as she could.

"Warren!" she whispered, aware that the gang was still within earshot. "Warren, wake up! Wake up!"

She crouched down and shook Warren's body. Nothing. She shook it again, and again. Still nothing.

"Oh God, Warren!" she said, this time more loudly.

And then, slowly, Warren's eyes began to open. Relief overcame her for the second time that week.

"Warren, I thought they'd, I thought they'd..."
Warren suddenly sat bolt upright as if nothing had happened. He had all the life back in him as if someone had pushed a **switch** marked 'on'.
"Run away!" he whispered to Lorna urgently. "Leave! Quickly! Now! They might see you!"
"But Warren, you..."
"Lorna, go! Just go! If they see you they'll kill you! I'm a danger to you!"
Warren's voice changed from concern to anger, and the look of urgency on his face could not be mistaken. He was not confused and he wasn't joking. He was deadly serious.
Lorna's eyes began to fill with tears.
"Warren, please! I need to help..."
"For Christ's sake, Lorna, get away from me!" he ordered her.
He was still whispering, but Lorna felt his rage as if he had screamed the command from the very bottom of his lungs.
Lorna's relief had been short-lived, and now she was totally shocked and confused. Her **attachment** to Warren was so much greater than she had even realized herself, just quarter of an hour earlier, in the car, on her way to meet him. It was a deep desire to protect him that had only **surfaced** when he was being attacked. And now the thought of leaving him there in the street quite simply **crushed** her heart. But the look in Warren's eyes told her she had no option – it was a look of pure anger at her presence.
Lorna stood up. It took all of her strength to stay silent, but she did. She carefully stepped back into the shadows and walked as quietly as possible back to the car park. Lorna desperately wanted to look back, but she held herself together and stopped herself from doing so. She knew that if she looked back, the sight would tear her apart.

switch	Schalter
attachment	emotionale Verbundenheit
to surface	hochkommen
to crush	zerdrücken
to growl	knurren

Before she could even reach the entrance to the car park, Lorna was physically pulled away from her thoughts. Without any warning, a hand grabbed her arm and, before Lorna could scream, a second hand covered her mouth. Lorna felt herself being pulled away from the pavement and behind a wall. She struggled, trying desperately to free herself from the hands, but they were so big and gripped her so tightly that it was useless. The man was holding her back against him, so she could not see who it was. Terrified, she tried again and again to scream. Still (i) no sound could pass the enormous hand covering her mouth. Then a familiar voice **growled** in her ear.

> **Still** hat unterschiedliche Bedeutungen, z. B.: noch, ruhig, bewegungslos.
>
> Hier bedeutet es „dennoch".

Übung 32: Questions. Beantworten Sie die Fragen zum Text in ganzen Sätzen!

1. Why was Warren lying motionless on the pavement?

   ____

2. From where did Lorna witness the confrontation?

   ____

3. Why did Warren urge Lorna to leave as fast as possible?

   ____

4. Why did Lorna not look back as she walked away?

   ____

civil	*hier:* höflich
to loosen one's grip	seinen Griff lockern
to appease	besänftigen
fate	Schicksal
expressionless	ausdruckslos

"Now don't tell me *that* was a misunderstanding."
The man pulled her round so she could see his face, and slowly took his hand away from her mouth.
"Ian!" Lorna said, not screaming, but still with panic in her voice. "What the hell do you think you're doing? You scared me half to death!"
"I've tried being civil. I've tried being reasonable. But still you refuse to tell me the truth. I figured that following you was the only way of getting the truth. And it seems you've led me right to it."
Lorna was speechless. What the hell was she supposed to do now?
"Ian... you... you followed me?"
"Well, it wasn't difficult, Lorna. I mean, if you're going to go out somewhere dressed up like that and *not* be seen, next time try leaving the house a bit more discreetly."
Ian now gripped Lorna's arms with both of his hands. Her arms were beginning to really hurt.
"Please," she begged him. "You're hurting me, Ian!"
Ian loosened his grip, but didn't let go completely.
"Did one of those men hurt Katie?" he asked, firmly.
Lorna swallowed, but as she did she suddenly had a brainwave – and it was Ian who had given it to her. Maybe there was a way to appease Ian *and* protect Warren. And maybe, just maybe, she might save a group of poor, poor girls from an unthinkably dark fate. Yes, she thought. This is the only way.
After a few seconds, she nodded her head slowly. "Yeah. It was the tall one. The one with the spiky black hair and long black coat."
"Finally," Ian sighed satisfied. "What's his name?"
What had Warren called him? Lorna tried desperately to remember. It took her a couple of seconds, but luckily, Ian thought she was hesitating only because she didn't want to give him the name.

Übung 33: Word spiral. Finden Sie die Lösungswörter und tragen Sie sie in die Wortspirale ein!

1	2	3	4	5	6	7
22	23	24	25	26	27	8
21	36	37	38	39	28	9
20	35	42	41	40	29	10
19	34	33	32	31	30	11
18	17	16	15	14	13	12

1-9: The town in northern England where Lorna and Katie live.
9-15: A tough material produced from the skin of animals.
15-24: The leader of a gang.
24-27: To do something quickly and a little hectically.
27-30: When you die, you either go to heaven or ________.
30-32: What you do when you don't tell the truth.
32-35: People who go to (27-30) are ________.
35-42: A person who teaches at a university.

"Hurry up!" he growled.
"He's called Rory."
"And where can I find this 'Rory'?"
Lorna swallowed again. "On Granville Road. He and the others are going there now."
Ian let go of Lorna's arm. Suddenly he was quite calm, his face **expressionless**, and he simply said: "Thank you, Lorna. Finally I can put things right."
Then he turned and disappeared into the darkness, leaving Lorna standing alone in astonishment.

5 Hunting the Hunter

For perhaps ten seconds, Lorna stood completely still. Ian seemed to have vanished into thin air, and in the darkness, everything around her was unfamiliar. It felt as if she had slipped into some parallel fantasy world.

Then suddenly reality and the seriousness of the situation hit her with full force. She had just sent her sister's boyfriend right into the hands of a gang of evil, ruthless and murderous supernatural creatures.

As panic took command of her body, she felt her entire body beginning to shake. She had to lean against the wall in the multi-storey car park in order to stay upright.

Her breathing and her pulse were too fast. She realized she was hyperventilating, so she forced herself to take slow, deep breaths. This seemed to help and she began to calm down, which allowed her to think rationally.

She had to do something, and quickly, before it was too late. Ian had followed her, which meant he had also come in his car. Therefore he, too, had probably parked in the car park and there was a good chance that he had gone back to his car now. The best thing to do was to go to the exit and wait there for him to come out... if he came out. She had to try and stop him.

As she walked over to the exit, Lorna reached into her handbag and took out her mobile phone. She quickly found Ian's number and pressed 'dial'. The message 'Phone battery low!' flashed up on the screen and Lorna cursed herself for not recharging her phone the night before. Ian's voice came from the other end immediately; the phone did not make a single ringing-tone.

"Ian, listen..." Lorna began, but then, to her frustration, she realized the voice that had answered was pre-recorded.

ruthless	erbarmungslos
to recharge	wieder aufladen
ϟ to snap sb. out of sth.	jmd. aus etw. aufschrecken
slope	*hier:* Rampe

"Hi, it's Ian. Leave a message and I'll ring you back. Cheers."

"Ian, it's[i] Lorna," she said, rushing her words. "Ring me as soon as you get this. Do NOT go to Granville Road, Ian. It's extremely dangerous. Honestly, this is really important. You have to trust me. Do not go near that road. Just ring me, okay?"

Lorna put the phone down and began to bite one of her fingernails. She slowly walked into the car park, hoping desperately that Ian's familiar red sports car would appear driving towards her.

While she walked, she looked for Warren's phone number in her phone. Part of her wanted to go back outside and look for him, in case he was still nearby. She couldn't help worrying about him after his violent encounter with the vampire gang, but above all, she needed him by her side. He was, she thought as she took in a deep breath, the only one who could help her.

Im Gegensatz zum Deutschen meldet man sich am Telefon auf Englisch nicht mit „Hier ist ..." sondern mit "This is/It's ... (calling/speaking)".

But her more rational side told her that the street was still a dangerous place. What if the Midnight Hunters were still around? It was much safer to phone Warren, even if this meant using up more of her phone battery's precious power.

The sound of a car engine **snapped** Lorna **out of** her thoughts before she could call the mysterious boy she now cared so much about.

To Lorna's relief, she saw Ian driving down the **slope** from the first level. Things might not be as serious as she had feared.

Ian was using his mobile phone and Lorna had to wave at him so that he didn't drive straight past her. He slowed down to a standstill then opened his window.
"Okay, babe, I've got to go," he said, bringing his telephone conversation to an end. "Yeah, just... just... I'll explain later. I'll see you soon.... I love you, too. Bye."
"Ian, listen," Lorna said, the second he had ended the call. "You can't go to find that guy, Rory. It's dangerous. You don't know what..."
Ian interrupted her. "Lorna, just go home. I know what I'm doing."
"But you don't, Ian! That's the thing! You think you can take anyone on, but those men are..."
"Are you saying I can't take care of my own girlfriend? Are you saying that guy should hurt my baby and get away with it?"
"No, Ian, I'm not!" Lorna cried back. "But what if..."
How could she convince Ian? Was everything she said an attack on his masculinity? She decided to try another tactic.
"But what if you get the wrong guy?"
"Whether or not it was him, I don't think there's much chance of me getting the wrong guy," Ian replied as he put his car back into gear. "Now if you don't mind, I've got places to go."
"Just listen to me, Ian!"
"No, I won't listen!" Ian shouted back. "'Cos all you do is bloody lie."
"Ian!" Lorna screamed, but it was useless – Ian's electric window was closing.
Ian then turned his car stereo on and turned up the sound to full volume, pumping out the heavy bass of a dance track.
Lorna banged on the car window, but Ian ignored her. He began to pull away. She pulled at his door handle but the door was locked. Ian accelerated and she was forced to let go of the handle.
"Ian! Ian!" she shouted after him, but her cries were in vain.

gear	Gang (Auto)
to pump out	*hier:* dröhnen
to accelerate	Gas geben
in vain	vergebens
literally	buchstäblich

Ian was out of the car park and turning left into Wellington Road. She still had her mobile phone firmly grasped in her hand. Calling Ian was useless. Now Warren was her only hope. While she hurried up to level one where her own car was parked, she selected the vampire's name on her mobile. The message 'Phone battery low!' once again flashed up on the screen.

After the fourth ring, Warren answered.

"Lorna, are you okay?" he said, without as much as a 'hello'.

"I don't know, Warren. You've got to help me!"

"What is it, Lorna? I thought you were safe? I followed the gang to be sure that they..."

"Yeah, I'm safe, but... oh God, I've done something terrible, Warren!" The more she spoke out loud, the more she became filled with panic once again. "I told Ian, Katie's boyfriend, that Katie was attacked by the vampire who punched you. The one called Rory. Now Ian's gone to Granville Road to confront him. I wanted to protect you, Warren. I just..."

"What?" Warren cried at the other end of the line. "He can't mess with Rory! Rory will kill him! **Literally**, he'll kill him, Lorna!"

"I know, I know!" Lorna cried, her voice breaking down more and more with each word.

"Okay, listen. Stay calm," Warren ordered. "Just tell me exactly what happened. When did you last see Ian?"

"He drove away from the car park just a minute ago. I tried my best to stop him, but it was useless," Lorna said, trying hard to speak clearly through her despair.

"And did Ian say he would go to Granville Road straight away?"

"I think so," Lorna answered. "Oh Warren, he was so furious..."

"Well, I'll be there before him, don't worry."

"But what are you going to..." Lorna began, but she was interrupted – not by Warren, but by a 'beep' from her phone to signal that her battery was almost completely flat.

"Just leave that to me," Warren answered. "I promise I'll sort things out. Phone Ian, Lorna, and try to convince him to stay away. It's very important. But more important still: you promise me you'll go straight home now. Do not stop for anything. Do you understand?"
"But Warren... the vampires... you might get..."
"I'm a vampire, too, Lorna. I can **stand up to** the Midnight Hunters."
When Warren said the words 'Midnight Hunters', Lorna felt goose pimples cover her skin. The gang's name added yet another dimension of danger.

to stand up to sb.	es mit jmd. aufnehmen, sich gegen jmd. behaupten
queue	Warteschlange
cleavage	Dekolleté

"Please, be careful!" Lorna begged Warren.
"I will be. But more importantly, *you* be careful. Go straight home and wait for me to call. I'll speak to you later."
Warren said goodbye and a moment later Lorna's lifeline seemed once again to be cut away from her.

Warren had to get to Granville Road as quickly as possible. There was no doubt about it – Katie's boyfriend's life was in real danger, and it was his duty to protect him. Warren set off through the streets, roads and alleyways of Blackpool.
After a few minutes, he reached Church Street. Groups of friends, dressed for a night on the town, walked up and down the pavements on either side of the road. Outside the Blackpool Winter Gardens, the town's famous concert hall, a long **queue** of teenagers stood waiting in excitement to be admitted into the building.
Seeing the young girls with their low cut tops, displaying their necks and **cleavages**, made Warren hungry. A week earlier, this hunger for blood would have felt natural, but now it seemed somehow perverse. He crossed the road, hurried past the queue of young people, and continued towards Granville Road.

Übung 34: Homonyms. Im Englischen gibt es viele Homonyme - Wörter, die mehrere Bedeutungen haben. Eine der vier Bedeutungen ist jeweils falsch - kreuzen Sie sie an!

1. mobile
   a) ❒ Handy
   b) ❒ beweglich
   c) ❒ Rasenmäher
   d) ❒ Mobile

2. ring
   a) ❒ Flügel
   b) ❒ Ring
   c) ❒ Klingeln
   d) ❒ Kreis

3. straight
   a) ❒ direkt
   b) ❒ streunend
   c) ❒ gerade
   d) ❒ heterosexuell

4. punch
   a) ❒ Kasper
   b) ❒ Dummkopf
   c) ❒ Punsch
   d) ❒ Faustschlag

Lorna's short journey home seemed to take forever. Every traffic light seemed to be red, and it felt as if every taxi in the city had decided to drive into the town centre at exactly the same time.
Lorna's car was like a bubble which separated her from the everyday world and kept her firmly in the supernatural one. Lorna wasn't driving through the heart of a partying city. She was right in the middle of a real-life nightmare, which was racing towards its murderous climax.
She had tried to ring Ian again. And then again. But each time Ian's recorded voice answered the call, and her phone reminded her that her battery was almost empty.

Then, while she was waiting at a red traffic light and feeling quite desperate, her phone began to ring.
"Thank God!" Lorna said to herself, but then noticed that it wasn't Ian. It was her mother.
Lorna answered the call. And as soon as she heard her mother's voice, she knew the news wasn't good.

Just minutes after he had passed the Winter Gardens, a faint sound caught Warren's attention. It was the sound of familiar voices a couple of streets away.
"Look, you shouldn't have said anything to Rory," came one voice. "Next time keep your mouth shut."
"Piss off!" came a reply. "It was just a joke. It was so funny to see his face when that bird ran away just because of his clothes and hair, before he'd even done anything! I thought he'd find it funny."
"Don't be an idiot! He would never find your stupid comments funny," came a third voice. "You said you could have done a hundred times better; basically you insulted his whole hunting method. Rory's always been sensitive about the way he hunts. You might think it's funny that the bird got away, but he takes it seriously."
"So what now?" came yet another voice. "I'm bloody hungry. I was looking forward to sucking dry a chick before J.P. messed things up. Anyone got any ideas where the five of us could go?"
Warren had no doubt about it – the voices were coming from the Midnight Hunters. But not all of them. Rory was missing. Where was he? What had happened?

faint	schwach
ϟ bird	*hier:* Tusse, Puppe
basically	im Grunde genommen
to insult	beleidigen
ϟ slut	Schlampe
ϟ to make mincemeat out of sb.	Hackfleisch aus jmd. machen

"Well, Rory's hunting on Granville Road," said the first voice. "And I think it's quite clear that he doesn't want any of us to join him tonight, so obviously we can't go there. Let's head towards the Pleasure Beach. There are some dark streets around there. It's good hunting ground."
"Ah, the Pleasure Beach," came the voice of the fifth of the vampires. "I can't wait to get my fangs into some stupid bird. The **sluts** round there deserve it. How I've missed Blackpool."
The voices were getting quieter. The vampires were walking away. Warren had to continue. He didn't have time to spare. Although it appeared that Rory was alone, the danger Ian faced was no less real. If Warren didn't get to Granville Road in time, the leader of the Midnight Hunters would **make** very bloody **mincemeat out of** Katie's boyfriend.

Übung 35: Verb forms. Lesen Sie weiter und ergänzen Sie die fehlenden Verben in der richtigen Form!

cry | be | argue | not know | mean | do

"Katie's gone? What **1.** ______ you ______ ?!" Lorna **2.** ______ down the phone to her mother.

"She's disappeared with Ian!" Mrs Irvine replied. "And now I **3.** ______ what the hell **4.** ______ ! I **5.** ______ in the bathroom and I could hear Katie and Ian **6.** ______ loudly downstairs. Then I heard Katie screaming!"

"Oh my God, Mum..."
"By the time I was downstairs, Ian was driving away with her in his car. And I could still hear her screaming from in there! And now I'm sick with worry. Dad's still in Lancaster, so I don't have a car. I have no idea what to do. I tried to phone Katie, but her phone's in her bedroom here, and I tried phoning Ian, but..."
Then the line went dead. Lorna looked down at her phone. The screen was black. Battery dead.
"Argh!" Lorna cried out, hitting the **steering wheel** in frustration.
A car's horn sounded behind her. She looked up and saw that the traffic light was green. She put her car into gear and pulled away.
Tears rolled down her cheeks as she drove down the road.
She remembered Ian's words. 'There's no chance of me getting the wrong guy.' Of course. There was no chance of getting the wrong guy, because he would take Katie – the victim and the witness – with him. But he knew that Katie didn't remember anything from the Halloween night! Didn't he even trust his own girlfriend?
Things wouldn't be like Ian had planned. Katie wouldn't recognize her attacker. Seeing Rory's face wouldn't **trigger** any memories. But then it would be too late. They would have taken a step too far into the vampire world. And Ian's usual, violent way of solving a problem would be useless.
By sending Ian to Granville Road, Lorna had sent Katie, too. Her sister had experienced and survived a violent vampire attack in the past week, and now Lorna was responsible for pushing her down this path all over again! Except there was no bright light at the end this time. This time, survival was almost certainly impossible.
Everything was going wrong, so, so wrong, Lorna thought, fighting against her tears. And she, herself, was to blame.

steering wheel	Lenkrad
to trigger	auslösen, hervorrufen

Übung 36: Match-up. Verbinden Sie die Satzteile, um sinnvolle Sätze zu schaffen!

1. ☐ Mrs Irvine didn't have the car...
2. ☐ The driver behind Lorna sounded his horn...
3. ☐ Mrs Irvine couldn't speak to Katie...
4. ☐ Lorna's conversation with her mother was cut off...

a) because the traffic light was green.

b) because her phone battery was dead.

c) because her phone was in her bedroom.

d) because Mr Irvine was in Lancaster.

Above Warren's head the sign read 'Granville Road'. The road was rather badly lit, with just a few **lampposts** struggling to throw out any light. It was quite a long road, with an **industrial yard** on one side and old **semi-detached houses** on the other.

lamppost	Laternenpfahl
industrial yard	Industriegelände
semi-detached house	Doppelhaus-hälfte
smoothly	reibungslos

Warren could see why it was ideal hunting ground for Rory and the gang. It was quiet enough for any attack to go unnoticed. But the quietness didn't mean that the shadows were empty.

Warren walked into the shadows himself and headed down the street.

When the roads became clearer and the traffic started to flow more **smoothly**, Lorna began to drive towards Granville Road. Going

home wasn't an option now. There was simply no time. She had to go after Katie, even if Warren had told her to stay away.
She drove fast – faster than was really safe – and her car's little green digital clock told her that it was 10:13 when she arrived.
Sitting in her car, looking down the street, Lorna could see little more than shadows. Vehicles were parked on both sides of the road and trees **lined** the pavements. But when Lorna spotted a red sports car about twenty metres down the road, she knew it could only belong to one person. Ian.

to line	*hier:* säumen
weapon	Waffe
to creep	schleichen

It was only now that she realized she had absolutely no idea what to do. If she drove down the street, Rory would see her immediately. Far from ideal. But if she walked in the shadows next to the road, she was completely unprotected (i).
Either bravely or stupidly, Lorna decided that going on foot, from shadow to shadow, was the only real option. Driving down and being spotted straight away wouldn't help anyone.
She parked her car and looked around her in desperate but unrealistic hope that she would find some kind of **weapon**. But there was nothing she could use. She took a long, slow breath in, breathed out, then locked her car and walked back to Granville Road.
The road was still quiet and filled with shadows. Lorna moved as quietly as possible, from shadow to shadow, towards Ian's car.
When she was about ten metres away, the driver's door opened, and Ian stepped out. He turned his head and quietly spoke to someone still inside the car, and then he began to walk into the middle of the road.

Un- ist auch im Englischen eine häufig verwendete negative Vorsilbe, ebenso wie **dis-**(agree), **im-**(possible), **in-**(credible), **il-**(legal).

"Ian!" Lorna said in a whisper; a whisper that wasn't loud enough to catch his attention. "Ian!" she tried again.
But still it was useless, he was already on the other side of the street.

Übung 37: If-sentences. Ergänzen Sie die fehlenden Verbformen!

1. Do you think she say yes ________________ if I ask ________________ her out on a date?
2. If she leave ________________ home tomorrow, I miss ________________ her so much.
3. Do you know what, I not go ________________ to work if I win ________________ the lottery.
4. If I see ________________ a vampire, I definitely be ________________ scared, no question about it!

Lorna **crept** closer to the car, until she could see her twin sister's face in the sports car's passenger seat. She continued until she was at the driver's door, then as quietly as possible, she opened the door and climbed inside, unnoticed by Ian.
Katie, of course, noticed the door opening, and Lorna had to warn her immediately not to make a sound.
"Shhhhhhh, Katie!" she said in a whisper with one finger over her mouth. "We need to stay quiet. I'll explain everything, but you have to do exactly what I say. Just trust me."
Katie seemed relieved to see Lorna. She pointed across the road and whispered: "Ian said that guy attacked me in the club. But I wasn't attacked, Lorna, I know I..."
Katie was interrupted. Ian had begun to shout in the street.

"Oi! You! You by the gate! Get over here, now!"
Now Lorna knew that the street was not empty at all. She saw exactly whom Ian was shouting at. Standing in the shadows, by a huge black gate, was the ringleader of the Midnight Hunters. The gate was open and led into an industrial yard. It seemed to **camouflage** Rory in his black coat and boots.
"Are you ignoring me, freak? I said, get... out... here... NOW!"
The vampire gave a short, sharp reply, but from within the car, the response was **inaudible**. Then Rory stepped out from the side of the gate, and a streetlight illuminated the black spikes on the top of his head. He walked right up to Ian, until he was just a metre away on the pavement, opposite the girls in the car.
Lorna's head was spinning. Was there nothing she could do? And where was Warren? He'd said he'd be there.

to camouflage	tarnen
inaudible	unhörbar
pathetic	jämmerlich, lächerlich

"And what do *you* want?" asked the Midnight Hunter in his aristocratic voice.
Lorna noticed that Katie's window was open a couple of centimetres. They had to remain completely silent to avoid being heard, but at least with the vampire so close the girls could hear him speak.
"I want to show you that nobody messes with me or my Katie, you sick, perverted piece of shit," Ian replied.
"Pardon?" Rory looked slightly confused, but not intimidated. If anything, he looked amused at Ian's stupidity.
Ian's reply was not vocal but physical. He swung his right arm round to punch Rory, just as Rory had done to Warren earlier in the evening. But Ian's punch was **pathetic** in comparison to Rory's lightning-fast reaction. He grabbed Ian's fist with his left hand and punched Ian in the stomach with his right.
"Oh-orrrr!" came Ian's cry of pain.

Rory punched Ian again, this time in the head. Ian fell backwards onto the boot of a parked car, and then rolled off the car and fell to the ground.
"Ian!" Katie exclaimed in the car.
But, as tired and weak as she was and in a state of utter shock and confusion, she made almost no sound.

boot	Kofferraum
to pick a fight	einen Streit vom Zaun brechen

Warren had been watching the unequal fight. Now he stepped out of the shadows.
"Leave him alone, Rory!" he commanded.
Warren's sudden arrival surprised Rory enough to make him hold back from kicking Ian again. Rory turned to Warren.
"Warren! How wonderful!" he said in his usual sarcastic voice. "You've accepted my invitation to join me!"
"Just leave, Rory. Please. You don't want to pick a fight here."
"Wait a second... Let me get this right. You're protecting this thug who appeared from nowhere and started to pick a fight with me?"
Warren knew exactly why he had to protect Ian. Two much more vulnerable and important people were sitting in the red sports car, just metres from where the fight had broken out. Warren had smelt Lorna coming down the street and then seen her climb into the driver's seat next to her sister. Why hadn't she followed his orders and gone straight home? Did she really not realize how dangerous it was for her to be there?
Warren wasn't scared of Rory, but he was terrified of what would happen if Rory saw – or smelt – the two young, beautiful girls who were also witnessing the confrontation. Protecting them was his priority. If he could distract Rory for a while, it would give Ian the chance to get back to the car, then hopefully all three humans would drive to safety. It wasn't a perfect plan, but it was the best he had.
Warren took a deep breath.

"I've no idea who this guy is," he lied. "I wanted to talk to you, and… apologize for before. I shouldn't have said what I did. But how can I talk to you when you're ripping some guy to pieces?"
"Warren, did nobody ever tell you that you're a terrible liar? You expect me to believe that you want to give me a sincere, heart-felt apology? Don't insult my intelligence."
Warren realized with relief that Ian, who was lying on the ground behind Rory, was still conscious, despite the beating he had received. With his bloody face and battered body, he was now starting to crawl towards the red sports car.
Warren looked Rory straight in the eye. "You really think I'm 'Good Little Warren', don't you? Do you really think that I left the Hunters to become some hero, some saint? You don't think that I have my weaknesses, too?"
"I don't know what the hell you're talking about, Warren," Rory replied, with a look of absolute seriousness on his face. "But if you really want to start some long, heart-breaking monologue about your personal struggle, we might want to find some privacy."
Rory glanced at Ian, who was almost at the passenger door of the car. Then he looked back to Warren and continued.
"I've finished with him, anyway." He then lowered his voice, to be sure that Ian would not hear. "I enjoy a much sweeter taste than a man could offer, anyway. Whatever you have to say, keep it short. I'm here to hunt. It's a word that you don't really understand."
Warren began to talk about his moral struggle, going back to the old days, back when he was a hunter. But every word he said was nonsense, and he suspected that Rory knew this.

liar	Lügner
battered	zerschlagen
crawl	*hier:* kriechen (auf allen Vieren)
saint	Heiliger
struggle	Kampf
sinister	böse, unheimlich

Übung 38: Unscramble the words. Lesen Sie weiter, ordnen Sie den Buchstabensalat zu sinnvollen Wörtern und ergänzen Sie die Lücken im Text!

hsieadltgh | sspngaree | engirest | lleh | igneen | spimrave

To Warren's relief, the sound of a car 1. _____ interrupted the two 2. _____ . Both turned towards the red sports car. Despite the bright 3. _____ shining in his eyes, Warren could see Katie behind the 4. _____ wheel and Ian in the 5. _____ seat. So where the 6. _____ was Lorna?!

Katie began carefully to drive the powerful car into the road.
"You... bloody liar!" Rory said to Warren in disgust. "That's the girl from the club! You knew her?!"
Warren didn't reply. He just stood watching the car. Now Katie had pulled out and was driving away, down Granville Road. But what about Lorna? Her scent was still in the air.
"I don't like liars," Rory continued, in an icy-cold, **sinister** voice. "I don't like liars one bit."
Then with a terrible, evil expression on his face and a quiet, macabre laugh, he pulled a long knife out of his deep coat pocket.
"Liars need to be taught a lesson," he said in a whisper, and then, with his usual lightning speed, he swung the knife towards Warren's head. This time, Warren reacted with equal speed to Rory and jumped to his right, away from the huge knife.

But a second later, Rory was coming for him again. He swung the **blade** at Warren's side and Warren jumped down to the ground, trying desperately to escape this psychotic vampire. A second later he was back on his feet, but with the industrial yard fence behind him, he had nowhere to go.

blade	Klinge
hilarious	urkomisch
to underestimate	unterschätzen
sb.'s heart sinks	jmd. rutscht das Herz in die Hose
acting	Schauspielerei

Rory was now laughing arrogantly, but also almost manically, as if he found the situation quite **hilarious**!

I knew he was sick bastard, Warren thought to himself, but I never knew he was actually mad!

"You're not good enough for a vampire existence," Rory began, standing just a metre away from Warren now.

His knife was now down by his side, and Warren spotted a perfect opportunity to attack. Quick as a flash, he raised his right leg and kicked at Rory's arm, hoping to kick away his knife. But Warren's plan didn't work. He had completely **underestimated** the speed of the powerful ringleader's reactions. Rory swung his arm back, avoiding Warren's kick, and then swung it back round at Warren's leg.

"Argh!" Warren cried, feeling a sharp pain hit his knee. "You bast..."

"No!" came a girl's scream from the other side of the road.

Warren's **heart sank**. His fear had become a reality: Lorna had stepped into the path of Rory's rage.

Lorna felt the vampire's eyes cut through the darkness like a knife, and it seemed as if his stare alone might kill her.

Behind Rory, Warren now lay on the floor. For a few seconds he cried out in pain, but then he fell silent and was still. Now, with Rory facing her, Lorna felt completely helpless. Rory began to walk towards her, but like a rabbit caught in the headlights of a coming car, she didn't move. He was still holding his knife, but it was down by his side.

Rory was within arm's reach. But he didn't open his mouth and show her his fangs. Instead, he gently put his head at the side of hers and whispered in her ear.
"Tell me, are you scared?"
Lorna silently nodded her head.
Rory laughed. "You think this is fear? You think this is horror? You don't know a thing. But I think I can teach you. While I get to satisfy my hunger, you get to understand what fear *really* means."

Übung 39: Questions. Beantworten Sie die folgenden Fragen zum Text!

1. Why did Rory want to teach Warren a lesson?

   ____

2. When Warren had his back to the industrial yard, how did Rory react?

   ____

3. Why did Warren's plan to kick away the knife not work?

   ____

4. Why did Warren's heart sink when he heard Lorna scream?

   ____

Warren was not unconscious, but his **acting** was good. And Rory, distracted now by this beautiful girl, full of sweet-smelling, perfumed blood, was no longer concentrating on Warren, who lay motionless on the ground. For the arrogant Rory, their battle was over and his fun was about to begin.

Rory was blocking Lorna's view, so she hadn't seen Warren stand up silently and walk in their direction. Now he stood directly behind Rory. His leg was bleeding badly, but he couldn't feel the pain. His love for Lorna and need to protect her gave him all the energy he needed.

Warren took a step back and then threw himself at the tall vampire, throwing punches to his head at the same time. It worked! The full force of Warren's weight with the added element of surprise and both men fell to the ground like domino stones, the knife flying from Rory's hand.

Warren pounced onto the ringleader and held his arms and legs down. Then he turned to Lorna, who still hadn't moved.

"Run!" he cried. "Run, and don't look back!"

"Get off me!" Rory demanded.

Warren knew that he couldn't hold Rory for long, and in that time Lorna had to escape. He turned back, hoping to see Lorna running as far down the street as possible. But no, Lorna was still there.

"Run!" he cried, but still Lorna stood there, staring at them. Warren knew that in a few seconds Rory would overpower him, and this time he wouldn't wait for a second to grab Lorna and take her. The threat to Lorna seemed greater than ever, and Warren was almost overcome by his fear for her life as it exploded inside him. But suddenly, this fear transformed into adrenaline with such violence that he himself was amazed by his sudden power.

With his left hand, he held Rory's neck to the ground, and with his right, he grabbed the knife. Without pausing for a second, he pressed the knife down on the Midnight Hunter's neck. A thin cut appeared in Rory's neck, followed by a small line of blood.

Rory was trying to swallow, but the pressure of the knife stopped him from doing so. Then he tried to speak, but this, too, was almost impossible with the knife so close to his voice box.

voice box	Kehlkopf
defeat	Niederlage

"Oh.... kay..." Rory struggled to say. "I was... wrong. I was... wrong. Just do it. Do it quickly. This is how it is to be."
Rory had accepted defeat. But that wasn't all, Warren realized. He had accepted death.
"Just do it!" he said again, still struggling with each word.
Warren looked into Rory's eyes and saw fear. For a vampire, this was the worst humiliation. To be scared was to lose self-respect. And without self-respect, he had no reason for existence.
Warren pressed the knife in harder, making the blood stream out faster. But he didn't want the blood of Rory's death on his hands.
Warren pulled the knife away, stood up, and threw his arms around Lorna, holding her whole body tight.

Übung 40: Similes and metaphors. Ergänzen Sie die fehlenden Vokabeln, um Vergleiche bzw. Metaphern zu schaffen.

1. On seeing the vampire, the man turned as white as a ________________.
2. The man leapt from the wall down onto the man and they both fell like ________________.
3. The man couldn't move. He simply stood there, perfectly still, like a ________________ caught in a car's headlights.
4. The girl's scream cut like a ________________ through the silence.

Rory slowly stood up and began to walk away. Then he paused and turned round. "You should have finished me off while you had the chance."
"Maybe I should have. Another time, perhaps..." Warren replied.
"Watch your back, Warren. The Midnight Hunters don't believe in mercy."
Then he turned away, and without a further word, he was gone.

mercy	Gnade, Erbarmen
to shiver	zittern, schaudern
eternity	Ewigkeit
from the bottom of one's heart	aus tiefstem Herzen

Lorna shivered. She was still in a state of shock, but with the immediate panic gone, she was feeling the cold for the first time. It felt like Warren's arms had been around her for an eternity. But, she realized when he pulled away, eternity wasn't long enough.
Lorna turned to face Warren. He, too, turned his head, and the two shared their second kiss. This time, neither Lorna nor Warren hesitated, and the kiss was loving and soft, tender and slow.
"I don't think I can stand your beauty any more, Lorna. Everything about you means happiness – your scent... it drives me crazy! I don't think you understand what this means."
"But... isn't that a good thing?"
"No, Lorna. That is why I have to leave," Warren continued, "I can't trust myself to leave your beauty untouched forever."
"But I trust you now, Warren. Doesn't that mean anything?"
The thought of Warren leaving filled her with fear and despair.
"It means everything to me. But trust alone won't keep you safe. Never forget how much..." Warren stopped and moved his lips without making a sound. But Lorna could read his lips: 'I love you.'
Warren moved his head towards Lorna's, and Lorna closed her eyes. It was a heartbreaking kiss.
"I love you, too," Lorna said, and opened her eyes.
But nobody had been there to hear her words. Warren was gone.

Lorna felt the pain of losing Warren in every cell of her body. But she no longer felt afraid. Despite the pain, she knew that he was right. He had saved her life, as well as her sister's, and she would be grateful to him, she knew, for the rest of her life. Lorna just hoped, **from the bottom of her** broken **heart**, that one day their paths would cross again.

Übung 41: Crossword. Lösen Sie das Kreuzworträtsel!

Across

1. Showing no pity, compassion or mercy.
4. The part of a knife which does the cutting.
5. What you have in your head when you think about the past.
6. A slang word to refer to a girl or woman.
8. A line of people waiting for something.

Down

2. Extremely funny.
3. ________ wheel – the part of a car used to go round corners.
7. Something you feel you have to do – it is right that you do it.

Abschlusstest

Übung 1: Definitions. Welches Wort ist gemeint?

1. a human who changes into a wolf ____________
2. a dangerous tool with teeth, powered by energy and used for cutting wood ____________
3. what you have the next day if you drink too much the night before ____________
4. what you walk along next to a road ____________

Übung 2: Word spiral. Finden Sie die Begriffe in der Wortspirale!

1	2	3	4	5	6	7
22	23	24	25	26	27	8
21	36	37	38	39	28	9
20	35	42	41	40	29	10
19	34	33	32	31	30	11
18	17	16	15	14	13	12

1-5: Seligkeit
5-9: scharf
9-12: Hafenmole
12-19: rücksichtslos
19-25: Schlange
25-30: Drohung
30-36: Donner
36-42: Gerüchte

Übung 3: Questions. Kreuzen Sie jeweils die richtige Antwort an!

1. What do Lorna and Helena study at university?
   - a) ❐ Sociology.
   - b) ❐ Business Studies.
   - c) ❐ Travel and Tourism Management.

2. On what date were Lorna and Katie born?
   - a) ❐ 31st October.
   - b) ❐ 1st November.
   - c) ❐ 2nd November.

3. What is Lorna's attitude towards Katie's boyfriend?
   - a) ❐ Lorna wishes Katie would find a nicer boy but will let her sister make her own mistakes.
   - b) ❐ Lorna thinks Katie and Ian make a perfect pair.
   - c) ❐ Lorna will do anything to try and split them up.

Übung 4: Match-up. Bilden Sie Phrasal Verbs!

1. ☐ to burst	a) a brainwave
2. ☐ to pour	b) one's teeth
3. ☐ to have	c) into tears
4. ☐ to grind	d) with rain

Übung 5: Word search. Finden Sie im Gitternetz acht Adjektive, die Lornas Gefühle im Laufe der Geschichte beschreiben!

E	M	B	A	R	R	A	S	S	E	D
B	A	S	N	H	A	P	P	C	P	O
T	S	K	X	G	H	V	A	A	U	S
Y	H	O	I	A	P	A	A	R	N	A
B	O	C	O	N	F	U	S	E	D	F
E	C	O	U	N	P	O	T	D	E	G
T	K	A	S	O	Z	I	O	O	F	O
A	E	Z	G	Y	E	W	U	L	L	X
O	D	P	R	E	L	I	E	V	E	D
E	Y	E	F	D	A	W	B	N	K	L
H	E	A	R	T	B	R	O	K	E	N

1. ______________________ 5. ______________________

2. ______________________ 6. ______________________

3. ______________________ 7. ______________________

4. ______________________ 8. ______________________

Übung 6: Since or for? Ergänzen Sie die fehlenden Präpositionen!

1. Katie was in a coma __________ almost three days.
2. When Lorna phoned Warren at Helena's house, she hadn't spoken to him __________ Monday that week.
3. Warren had known that Lorna was different __________ he saw her for the first time in Visage Club.
4. __________ a moment, Lorna stood completely still.

Übung 7: Places to go in Blackpool. Wie gut kennen Sie sich in Blackpool aus? Beantworten Sie die folgenden Fragen!

Where would you go if...

1. ...you wanted a traditional English breakfast in a little café?

   ____

2. ...you wanted to see a concert?

   ____

3. ...you wanted to spend an evening in some of the classier bars?

   ____

4. ...you wanted to watch the sunset?

   ____

Übung 8: Idioms. Ergänzen Sie die fehlenden Substantive und verbinden Sie die idiomatischen Ausdrücke mit der entsprechenden Bedeutung!

butterflies heart cards mincemeat

1. ☐ to make ______ out of someone
2. ☐ to keep one's ______ close to one's chest
3. ☐ to have ______ in one's stomach
4. ☐ from the bottom of one's ______

a) in a very intense or passionate way

b) to destroy someone

c) to keep information about one's intentions secret

d) to be very nervous

Übung 9: Quantifiers. Ergänzen Sie die fehlenden Bestimmungswörter „some" oder „any"!

1. Lorna wished that the DJ would play ______ good music.
2. "Have you heard ______ news from the hospital?"
3. Wellington Road offered ______ of the classier bars in Blackpool.
4. Lorna was glad that she didn't have ______ lectures.

Lösungen

Übung 1: **1.** werewolf **2.** chainsaw **3.** identical **4.** midnight

Übung 2: **1.** began **2.** jumped **3.** ran **4.** tried **5.** pushed **6.** wasn't **7.** lost **8.** fell

Übung 3: **1.** mummy **2.** speak **3.** bad **4.** little

Übung 4: **1.** richtig **2.** falsch (The deafening music filled the silence between Lorna and Warren.) **3.** falsch (Lorna blushed because it was clear that she was trying politely to end the conversation.) **4.** richtig

Übung 5: **1.** Lorna was kissed (by Warren). **2.** Their conversation was interrupted (by the mobile phone). **3.** After a few seconds, the silence was broken (by Warren).

Übung 6: **1.** seven **2.** centimetres **3.** doubt **4.** muscles **5.** blood-stained **6.** army

Übung 7: **1.** scarier, scariest **2.** duller, dullest **3.** more impressive, most impressive **4.** worse, worst

Übung 8: **1.** d **2.** b **3.** a **4.** c

Übung 9: **1.** lip **2.** silence **3.** weird **4.** fake **5.** scent **6.** confusion **7.** delight
Lösung: perfect

Übung 10: **1.** d **2.** c **3.** b **4.** a

Übung 11: **1.** Where is Katie? **2.** Whose hand is covered in blood? **3.** Where is Lorna taking Katie? **4.** What does Katie want to do?

Übung 12: **1.** b **2.** c **3.** b

Übung 13: **1.** there **2.** to **3.** knew **4.** led

Übung 14:

							1 M					
2 G	I	R	L	F	R	I	E	N	D			
							S				3 P	
					4 H	O	S	P	I	T	A	L
	5 C	R	I	M	E		A				R	
					A		G				E	
		6 Y	E	A	R		7 E	A	R		N	
					T						T	

Übung 15: **1.** c **2.** d **3.** b **4.** a

Übung 16: **1.** Warren felt despair. **2.** He was permitted to smoke in a covered area near the door to the car park. **3.** She was scared because she knew Ian could be violent.

Übung 17: Lorna, I know you are hiding something from me – don't deny it! I want to talk. Don't try to bullshit me. I'll ring you later. Ian

Übung 18: **1.** to **2.** – **3.** At **4.** outside **5.** with **6.** of

Übung 19: **1.** falsch (Lorna told Farai there were no news from the hospital.) **2.** richtig **3.** richtig **4.** richtig

Übung 20:

S	A	T	H	P	P	E	P	P	E	R
Z	A	G	L	E	H	B	L	I	Z	S
K	I	P	R	A	O	L	C	U	O	C
M	B	O	B	X	T	S	T	R	O	A
M	E	N	U	B	O	A	R	D	K	R
B	L	A	L	C	O	L	V	N	Q	F
E	T	A	B	L	E	T	M	L	J	L
O	R	A	N	G	E	J	U	I	C	E

Übung 21: **1.** suspicion, suspiciously **2.** neutrality, neutrally **3.** anger, angrily **4.** emotion, emotionally

Übung 22: **1.** senses **2.** smell **3.** something **4.** side **5.** slowly **6.** story

Übung 23: **1.** touch **2.** hit **3.** flying **4.** watching **5.** sitting **6.** holding

Übung 24: **1.** b **2.** a **3.** d **4.** c

Übung 25: **1.** The girl in the café **2.** Warren **3.** Mr Irvine **4.** Lorna

Übung 26: **1.** "It's been ages since we last met."
2. The stress is really taking its toll on her health.
3. He is keeping his cards close to his chest.
4. Do you fancy going dancing in that new club tonight?

Übung 27: **1.** somebody **2.** nothing **3.** anything **4.** something **5.** something

Übung 28: **1.** how's **2.** I'm **3.** thanks **4.** Katie's **5.** parents' **6.** that's

Übung 29: **1.** Das Gespräch war am Anfang etwas unangenehm.
2. Ich bin erleichtert, dass Katie aufgewacht ist.
3. Sollen wir uns beim Parkhauseingang treffen?
4. Lorna antwortete ohne zu zögern.

Übung 30: **1.** trousers **2.** flat **3.** autumn **4.** car park

Übung 31: **1.** swinged (swung) **2.** Warrens (Warren's) **3.** to (too) **4.** quickly (quicker) **5.** hitted (hit) **6.** become (became)

Übung 32: **1.** He was lying motionless on the pavement because Rory had hit him hard. **2.** Lorna witnessed the confrontation from behind a van. **3.** Warren urged Lorna to leave because he was scared the gang would see her. **4.** Lorna didn't look back because she knew the sight would tear her apart.

Übung 33:

[1] B	[2] L	[3] A	[4] C	[5] K	[6] P	[7] O
[22] D	[23] E	[24] R	[25] U	[26] S	[27] H	[8] O
[21] A	[36] E	[37] C	[38] T	[39] U	[28] E	[9] L
[20] E	[35] L	[42] R	[41] E	[40] R	[29] L	[10] E
[19] L	[34] I	[33] V	[32] E	[31] I	[30] L	[11] A
[18] G	[17] N	[16] I	[15] R	[14] E	[13] H	[12] T

Übung 34: **1.** c **2.** a **3.** b **4.** b

Übung 35: **1.** do you mean **2.** cried **3.** don't know **4.** to do **5.** was **6.** arguing

Übung 36: **1.** d **2.** a **3.** c **4.** b

Übung 37: **1.** would say yes, asked **2.** left, would miss **3.** wouldn't go, won **4.** saw, would definitely be

Übung 38: **1.** engine **2.** vampires **3.** headlights **4.** steering **5.** passenger **6.** hell

Übung 39: **1.** Rory thought Warren was a liar. **2.** He laughed arrogantly. **3.** Rory reacted quickly and avoided Warren's kick (Warren underestimated Rory's reaction speed). **4.** Warren was afraid that Rory might kill Lorna.

Übung 40: **1.** ghost **2.** domino stones **3.** rabbit **4.** knife

Übung 41:

	[1] R	U	T	[2] H	L	E	[3] S	S	
				I			T		
			[4] B	L	A	D	E		
				A			E		
[5] M	E	M	O	R	Y		R		
				I		[6] B	I	R	D
		[7] D		O			N		
	[8] Q	U	E	U	E		G		
		T		S					
		Y							

Abschlusstest

Übung 1: **1.** werewolf **2.** chainsaw **3.** hangover **4.** pavement

Übung 2:

1 B	2 L	3 I	4 S	5 S	6 H	7 A
22 P	23 E	24 N	25 T	26 H	27 R	8 R
21 R	36 R	37 U	38 M	39 O	28 E	9 P
20 E	35 E	42 S	41 R	40 U	29 A	10 I
19 S	34 D	33 N	32 U	31 H	30 T	11 E
18 S	17 E	16 L	15 K	14 C	13 E	12 R

Übung 3: **1.** c **2.** a **3.** a

Übung 4: **1.** c **2.** d **3.** a **4.** b

Übung 5:

E	M	B	A	R	R	A	S	S	E	D
B	A	S	N	H	A	P	P	C	P	O
T	S	K	X	G	H	V	A	A	U	S
Y	H	O	I	A	P	A	A	R	N	A
B	O	C	O	N	F	U	S	E	D	F
E	C	O	U	N	P	O	T	D	E	G
T	K	A	S	O	Z	I	O	O	F	O
A	E	Z	G	Y	E	W	U	L	L	X
O	D	P	R	E	L	I	E	V	E	D
E	Y	E	F	D	A	W	B	N	K	L
H	E	A	R	T	B	R	O	K	E	N

Übung 6: **1.** for **2.** since **3.** since **4.** for

Übung 7: **1.** The Full Muffin **2.** The Winter Gardens **3.** Wellington Road **4.** Blackpool Tower

Übung 8: **1.** b (mincemeat) **2.** c (cards) **3.** d (butterflies) **4.** a (heart)

Übung 9: **1.** some **2.** any **3.** some **4.** any

Glossar

ϟ = umgangssprachlich

to accelerate	Gas geben
accidentally	versehentlich
acquaintance	Bekanntschaft
acting	Schauspielerei
ages	eine Ewigkeit
ϟ all over the place	*hier:* durcheinander
ambition	Bestreben
annoyed	verärgert
anxiety	Angst
to appease	besänftigen
to appreciate	schätzen, zu schätzen wissen
to approach	zugehen auf, sich nähern
to arch	*hier:* spannen
artificial	künstlich
astonishment	Verwunderung
attachment	emotionale Verbundenheit
to attend	teilnehmen an
attentively	aufmerksam
attire	Kleidung
awkward	unangenehm, peinlich
bad temper	üble Laune
baggy	schlabberig
basically	im Grunde genommen
battered	zerschlagen
to be aware of sth.	sich einer Sache bewusst sein
to be capable of	zu etw. fähig sein

to be exposed to sb./sth.	jmd./etw. ausgesetzt sein
to be on one's guard	auf der Hut sein
to be struck by sth.	von etw. beeindruckt sein
to be wired up	an etw. angeschlossen sein
bewildered	verwirrt
ϟ bird	*hier:* Tusse, Puppe
blade	Klinge
to blame sb.	jmd. etw. übel nehmen
bliss	Seligkeit
bloodstained	blutbefleckt
blurred	verschwommen
to blush	erröten
bolt upright	kerzengerade
boot	Kofferraum
brainwave	Geistesblitz
bravely	mutig
bulb	Glühbirne
ϟ to bullshit sb.	jmd. Scheiß erzählen
to burst into tears	in Tränen ausbrechen
to bury	begraben
to camouflage	tarnen
to catch up with sb./sth.	jmd. einholen, etw. nachholen
chainsaw	Kettensäge
to chat	plaudern
chest	Brust(korb)
choked	krächzend
civil	*hier:* höflich
claw	Klaue
cleavage	Dekolleté
ϟ to click	sich auf Anhieb verstehen
cloth	Lappen
coffin	Sarg
to comfort	trösten
compassion	Mitgefühl
concerned	besorgt
conscience	Gewissen
contradictory	widersprüchlich

convenient	*hier:* praktisch
to cough	husten
counter	*hier:* Theke
covered	*hier:* überdacht
coward	Feigling
craving	Gelüst, Verlangen
crawl	*hier:* kriechen (auf allen Vieren)
to creep (crept, crept)	schleichen
ϟ creep	Widerling
to crouch down	in die Hocke gehen
to crush	zerdrücken
Cupid	Amor
curiously	neugierig
to curl	sich einrollen
to curse under one's breath	unterdrückt fluchen
to dare	wagen
to dash	rasen, sausen
deafening	ohrenbetäubend
defeat	Niederlage
degree	(Uni-)Abschluss
deliberately	mit Absicht
to deny	*hier:* abstreiten
to deserve	verdienen
despair	Verzweiflung
to despise	verachten
to dig (dug, dug)	*hier:* graben
dim	dämmrig, düster
disbelief	Fassungslosigkeit
disgust	Abscheu
to distract	ablenken
disturbed	beunruhigt
dizzy	schwindelig
doomed	verdammt
to dread	fürchten, jmd. graut vor
dull	langweilig, fade
elderly	älter
to emphasize	betonen
encounter	Begegnung

to endanger	gefährden
envelop	umhüllen
epiphany	Erleuchtung
equally	ebenso
eternity	Ewigkeit
eventually	endlich, schließlich
exhausted	erschöpft
expressionless	ausdruckslos
to fade away	schwinden
to fail to do sth.	etw. versäumen, etw. nicht tun
faint	schwach
fairytale	Märchen
faithful	treu
fake	unecht
to falter	stocken
familiar	vertraut, bekannt
ϟ to fancy doing sth.	Lust haben, etw. zu tun
fang	Reißzahn
to fasten one's seatbelt	sich anschnallen
fate	Schicksal
feast	Festmahl
to feel (felt, felt) sick	jmd. wird schlecht
fed up	genervt
fierce	wild, gefährlich
firm	*hier:* entschieden
first aid kit	Erste-Hilfe-Ausrüstung
to fit (fit, fit) in	sich anpassen
fit of rage	Wutanfall
flash of lightning	Blitz
to fling (flung, flung)	schleudern
forthcoming	bevorstehend
from the bottom of one's heart	aus tiefstem Herzen
fur	Fell
to gasp	nach Luft schnappen
to gather	sammeln
gear	Gang (Auto)
gentle	zart
genuine	authentisch, echt

ϟ to get (got, got) it	etw. kapieren
ϟ to get worked up	sich über etw. aufregen
ghoul	leichenfressender Dämon
to give (gave, given) off	*hier:* verströmen
to glance	einen Blick werfen
goose pimples *pl*	Gänsehaut
gorgeous	toll, umwerfend
gracefully	graziös
to grind one's teeth	mit den Zähnen knirschen
to grip	ergreifen, erfassen
to growl	knurren
guardian angel	Schutzengel
gulp	Schluck
hangover	Kater
to harm sb.	jmd. schaden, jmd. verletzen
hazel	(haselnuss)braun
to head	sich in eine Richtung bewegen, auf etw. zusteuern
headlight	Scheinwerfer
sb.'s heart sinks	jmd. rutscht das Herz in die Hose
hesitancy	Unschlüssigkeit
high	*hier:* Rausch
hilarious	urkomisch
hooded jumper/hoody	Kapuzenpulli
to hum	*hier:* summen
humiliated	gedemütigt
impressive	beeindruckend, imposant
inappropriate	unangemessen
inaudible	unhörbar
incident	Vorfall
industrial yard	Industriegelände
insensitive	unsensibel, taktlos
instantly	sofort
to insult	beleidigen
to intimidate	einschüchtern
intoxicating	berauschend
in vain	vergebens

irresistible	unwiderstehlich
to jingle	klimpern
⚡ Jog on!	Hau ab!
to judge	*hier:* einschätzen
⚡ juicy	pikant (wörtlich: saftig)
to keep one's cards close to one's chest	sich bedeckt halten
to knock	*hier:* stoßen
lamppost	Laternenpfahl
laser beam	Laserstrahl
⚡ to lead (led, led) sb. on	jmd. falsche Hoffnungen machen
to leap (leapt, leapt)	einen Satz machen
lecture	Vorlesung
lecturer	Dozent(in)
liar	Lügner(in)
life support	*hier:* lebenserhaltende Maßnahmen
to line	*hier:* säumen
to linger	zurückbleiben, sich halten
literally	buchstäblich
local election	Kommunalwahl
to loosen one's grip	seinen Griff lockern
to maintain	behalten, beibehalten
⚡ to make mincemeat out of sb.	Hackfleisch aus jmd. machen
⚡ mate	Kumpel
mercy	Gnade, Erbarmen
⚡ messed up	verkorkst
⚡ to mess with sb.	jmd. zum Narren halten
messy	zerzaust
mischievous	spitzbübisch, verschmitzt
to misjudge	falsch einschätzen
to moan	stöhnen
moving	rührend, ergreifend
muddled	verworren
multi-storey car park	Parkhaus
mummy	Mumie

to mutter	murmeln, murren
odd	seltsam
to offend	beleidigen
out of habit	gewohnheitsmäßig
overconfident	zu selbstsicher
pale	blass
palm	*hier:* Handfläche
paralysed	gelähmt
patch	*hier:* Revier
pathetic	jämmerlich, lächerlich
to pick a fight	einen Streit vom Zaun brechen
plain	unansehnlich
pointless	sinnlos
posture	Körperhaltung
to pounce	sich auf etw. stürzen
to pour with rain	in Strömen gießen
to pretend	so tun, als ob
proposal	Vorschlag
to prowl	herumstreifen, pirschen
puddle	Pfütze
to pump out	*hier:* dröhnen
ϟ to punch sb.'s lights out	jmd. bewusstlos schlagen
to put the kettle on	Wasser aufsetzen
queue	Warteschlange
to quiz	ausfragen
to recharge	wieder aufladen
reckless	gedankenlos, rücksichtslos
to recommend	empfehlen
to regain	wiedergewinnen
relief	Erleichterung
repulsion	Abscheu, Ekelgefühl
to resist	widerstehen
ringleader	Anführer
rough	grob
to rumble	*hier:* grollen
rumour	Gerücht
to run (ran, run) riot	durchdrehen, verrücktspielen
to rush	hetzen, hasten

ruthless	erbarmungslos
saint	Heilige(r)
to satisfy	befriedigen
scar	Narbe
scathing	vernichtend
scent	Duft
to seduce	verführen
semi-detached house	Doppelhaushälfte
serpent	Schlange
to set (set, set) off	losfahren, losgehen
shallow	oberflächlich
to shift	*hier:* sich (von der Stelle) bewegen
to shiver	zittern, schaudern
shot	*hier:* Kurzer (Schnaps)
sin	Sünde
sincerity	Aufrichtigkeit
sinister	böse, unheimlich
skimpy	knapp
to slam	schlagen, hauen
slope	*hier:* Rampe
ϟ slut	Schlampe
smoothly	reibungslos
smug	süffisant
ϟ to snap sb. out of sth.	jmd. aus etw. aufschrecken
to snarl	die Zähne fletschen, knurren
to snigger	hämisch kichern
to sob	schluchzen
spellbound	verzaubert
spike	Stachel
to spill (spilt, spilt)	verschütten
to spin (spun, spun)	*hier:* sich drehen
to spot	sichten, erblicken
to spy on sb.	jmd. nachspionieren
to squeeze	drücken
to stamp	stempeln
to stand up to sb.	es mit jmd. aufnehmen, sich gegen jmd. behaupten

steady	gleichbleibend
steering wheel	Lenkrad
sth.'s not worth it	etw. lohnt sich nicht
to stream	strömen
struggle	Kampf
to struggle	*hier:* Mühe haben
to suck	saugen
to surface	hochkommen
surroundings *pl*	Umgebung
suspicion	Verdacht
suspicious	*hier:* misstrauisch
to swallow	schlucken
to sway	schwanken
switch	Schalter
sympathy	Mitgefühl
tainted	befleckt, unrein
to take its toll on	Auswirkungen haben, seinen Tribut fordern von
to take one's mind off sth.	sich ablenken
take the opportunity	die Gelegenheit ergreifen
to taunt	quälen
to tear (tore, torn) sb. apart	*hier:* jmd. das Herz brechen
temper	Laune, Charakter
temptation	Versuchung
tenderness	Zärtlichkeit
tense	angespannt
terraced house	Reihenhaus
terrifying	furchteinflößend
text message	SMS
there is no point in doing sth.	es hat keinen Sinn, etw. zu tun
to threaten	drohen
through gritted teeth	mit zusammengebissenen Zähnen
thug	Schläger, Rowdy
to thump	hämmern
tights *pl*	Strumpfhose
toddler	Kleinkind
torn in two	*hier:* zwiegespalten

to trickle	rinnen
to trigger	auslösen, hervorrufen
to trouble	*hier:* beunruhigen
tube	*hier:* Schlauch
turmoil	Aufruhr
unbearable	unerträglich
unblemished	makellos
unconscious	bewusstlos
to underestimate	unterschätzen
uneasy	unbehaglich
upset	*hier:* bestürzt, betroffen
utterly	vollkommen, völlig
to vanish	verschwinden
vicious	bösartig
voice box	Kehlkopf
vulnerable	verwundbar
ward	(Krankenhaus-)Station
weapon	Waffe
weird	eigenartig
ϟ What on earth…!	Was zum Teufel…!
wheelchair	Rollstuhl
whiff	Duft(hauch)
to wink	zwinkern
wire	*hier:* Kabel
within earshot	in Hörweite
to witness	miterleben, Zeuge sein
witty	geistreich, schlagfertig
wrapped up well	warm eingepackt
to yell	brüllen
to zip up	den Reißverschluss zumachen

Verzeichnis der Übungen

	Schwerpunkt	Übung	Seite
1	Wortschatz	Unscramble the words	6
2	Grammatik	Simple past	8
3	Wortschatz	Odd one out	9
4	Textverständnis	True or false?	11
5	Grammatik	Passive verb forms	14
6	Wortschatz	Fill in the gaps	15
7	Grammatik	Comparatives and superlatives	18
8	Textverständnis	Unscramble the dialogue	20
9	Wortschatz	Find the solution	22
10	Wortschatz	Antonyms	25
11	Grammatik	Forming questions	26
12	Textverständnis	Multiple choice	30
13	Wortschatz	Homophones	34
14	Wortschatz	Crossword	38
15	Wortschatz	Synonyms	41
16	Textverständnis	Answer the questions	43
17	Wortschatz	Text messaging	46
18	Grammatik	Prepositions	47
19	Textverständnis	True or false?	50
20	Wortschatz	Word search	52
21	Wortschatz	Word forms	55

	Schwerpunkt	Übung	Seite
22	Wortschatz	Translation	56
23	Grammatik	Infinitive or present participle?	58
24	Wortschatz	Negating prefixes	60
25	Textverständnis	Indirect speech	62
26	Wortschatz	Idiomatic expressions	64
27	Grammatik	Indefinite pronouns	66
28	Grammatik	Apostrophes	70
29	Wortschatz	Translation	72
30	Wortschatz	Americanisms	74
31	Wortschatz	Correct the mistakes	78
32	Textverständnis	Questions	81
33	Wortschatz	Word spiral	83
34	Wortschatz	Homonyms	89
35	Grammatik	Verb forms	91
36	Textverständnis	Match-up	93
37	Grammatik	If-sentences	95
38	Wortschatz	Unscramble the words	99
39	Textverständnis	Questions	101
40	Wortschatz	Similes and metaphors	103
41	Wortschatz	Crossword	105

Abschlusstest

1	Wortschatz	Definitions	106
2	Wortschatz	Word spiral	106
3	Textverständnis	Questions	107
4	Wortschatz	Match-up	107
5	Wortschatz	Word search	108
6	Grammatik	Since or for?	109
7	Textverständnis	Places to go in Blackpool	109
8	Wortschatz	Idioms	110
9	Grammatik	Quantifiers	110